D0542321

Seeking our Place of Resurrection

A Celtic Pilgrimage of Prayer

Prepared by
Timothy J. Ray

Copyright © 2021 Timothy J. Ray
All rights reserved.
ISBN: 9798706535186

To
Shirley Blotkamp, John Dale and Brian Ramsay

soul-friends who encouraged me to continue traveling
along this path of prayer

Table of Contents

Preface   i

Acknowledgements   ii

Approaching the "Thin Places" of God's Love   1

The Prayer Sequences

Part 1   From Loss to Love   9

1.1 O Splendour of God's Face
- a prayer of gratitude for the Triune God's generosity   11

1.2 O Word of Might, That Springing Forth
- a prayer of gratitude and commitment to Jesus   17

1.3 Shamed and Shaken Sore With Terror
- a sinner's prayer of remorse   23

1.4 I Call On You To Save Me
- a prayer for redemption from sin   29

1.5 Loving Jesus, Hear Me Calling
- a sinner's plea for mercy and assistance   35

1.6 I Am Not Worthy, O God
- a prayer of humble contrition   41

1.7 Redeemer, Sole-Begotten Son, You Are My Hope
- a redeemed sinner's plea for divine aid   47

1.8 Holy God, Let My Tongue Be Free From Blame
- a loved sinner's prayer for continued aid   53

1.9 Jesus, My Love, My Saviour
- a loved sinner's prayer of praise and service   59

Part 2   From Disciple to Friend   65

2.1 Let Thanks Arise On Every Side
- a prayer on the Incarnation   67

2.2 Behold The Lamb! He Comes.
- a prayer on Jesus' nativity   73

2.3 Gentle Jesus, Fount Of Healing
- a prayer for spiritual guidance and renewal   79

2.4 Dear Redeemer, Loved And Loving
  • a prayer of praise for Jesus' redemptive mission   85
2.5 Hear Me, Christ, My King
  • a humble petition to enter God's Kingdom   91
2.6 The Victor, Christ, With Flag Unfurled
  • a prayer on the demands of following Jesus   97
2.7 You Are, O Christ, My Health And Light
  • a prayer in praise of Jesus' power and majesty   103
2.8 Oh, Kind Creator Of the Skies
  • a prayer of Christian fellowship   109
2.9 To The Fount Of Life Eternal
  • a prayer of praise and gratitude for Christ's love   115

Part 3   From Passion to Resurrection   121

3.1 Dear God Of Mercy And Of Power
  • a prayer of praise, gratitude and victory   123
3.2 Let Earth And Heaven Rejoice And Sing
  • a penitent's prayer on Jesus' Passion (Last Supper)   129
3.3 From Out The Ancient Garden Came
  • a penitent's prayer on Jesus' Passion (Gethesame)   135
3.4 My Eyes Should Fall In Grief
  • a penitent's prayer on Jesus' Passion (Trial)   141
3.5 You Gave Your Life Upon The Tree
  • a penitent's prayer on Jesus' death upon a cross   147
3.6 The Sad Disciples Sat In Gloom
  • a prayer of joy and surprise for Jesus' Resurrection   153
3.7 Most Clement Jesus, Tender King
  • a prayer of praise for Jesus' redemption of humanity   159
3.8 Eternal Builder Of The Skies
  • a petition for the Risen Jesus' continuing presence   165
3.9 O You Who Seek God To Find
  • a petition to live as a redeemed child of God   171

Additional Prayer Exercises
two contemplative considerations of the day

Considerations   179
A Morning Prayer of Encircling   181
An Evening Prayer of Review   184

Resources

Recommendations for Scriptural Readings   189
Some Suggestions Concerning Music   195

Preface

In my books on Christian spirituality, I have explored points of contact between the Celtic and Ignatian traditions in the belief that they share core tenets and illuminate each other through their different practices. I have drawn upon the beauty and lyricism of Celtic Christianity to provide the narrative for these efforts while relying upon the rigorous disciplines of Ignatian spirituality to create the structural framework for my writings. So, in addition to using Ignatian spiritual practices to illuminate the life-journey of a seminal Celtic saint, I developed various types of devotions and worship — including the adaptation of various forms of traditional Ignatian prayer — using source materials from the ancient Celtic church or its traditions that survived in popular culture through the centuries.

This book and my *Finding Your Place of Resurrection* series represent the culmination of my explorations as I employ Celtic resources to engage the core text of the Ignatian spiritual tradition: *The Spiritual Exercises of Ignatius of Loyola.* However, these books are intended to provide to different and distinct spiritual experiences. Because of the positive response to *The Carmichael Prayerbook,* I chose to present in this book the graces of the Ignatian exercises — the qualities or understandings asked of God at the beginning of prayer — in a series of prayer sequences. As such, these are prayers of "holy desires" that may be approached as discrete prayers or in various thematic clusters. On the other hand, the three books in my *Finding Your Place of Resurrection* series (which also include the prayer sequences collected in this book) offer a self-guided journey through the Ignatian exercises meant to be encountered as an integrated whole.

So, it is my hope that the prayer sequences of this book assist you in expressing your holiest desires to God. Whether you use them alone or in communion with others, these are prayers of the heart testifying both to our love of God and to our awareness of the depth of God's love for us. May they bless you and all the people you touch in your life.

Acknowledgements

The prayer sequences presented in this book were developed using material from the following public domain books, all of which are available on the Internet Archive:

• *Early Christian Hymns; translations of the verses of the most notable Latin writers of the early and middle ages* (1908) by Daniel Joseph Donahoe.

• *Early Christian Hymns, Series II: translations of the verses of the early and middle ages* (1911) by Daniel Joseph Donahoe.

• *Hymns of the Early Church* (1896) by John Brownlie.

• *The Irish "Liber hymnorum"*, Volume 2 (1908) by John Henry Bernard Robert Atkinson.

• *The Religious Songs of Connacht: A collection of poems, stories, prayers, satires, ranns, charms, etc.*, Volume One (1906) by Douglas Hyde.

• *The Religious Songs of Connacht: A collection of poems, stories, prayers, satires, ranns, charms, etc.*, Volume Two (1906) by Douglas Hyde.

• *The Story of Iona* (1909) by Edward Craig Trenholme.

Since these prayer sequences are adaptations of these sources — not transcriptions or translations — any fault in their literary quality lies with the author.

Approaching the "Thin Places" of God's Love

an introduction to these prayers of holy desires

Approaching the "Thin Places" of God's Love

an introduction to these prayers of holy desires

As it is understood in the Celtic tradition, pilgrimage involves traveling to those "thin places" in the world where the boundary between the spiritual and material realms is most diaphanous. In these locations, men and women of faith cannot help but be humbled as the experience of God and the divine comes effortlessly — almost with the ease of breathing. Yet, pilgrims and holy wanderers are meant to continue their journeys and visit other "thin places" where they also experience the presence of God in profound and deeply meaningful ways before finally arriving at their "place of resurrection".

As such, pilgrimage involves awareness of the presence of God in the present moment as well as memories of past experiences of God — making the pilgrim's life a journey of grace marked by a profound awareness of God's presence in his or her life. The joyful acknowledgment of this graced existence usually takes the form of prayer, whether expressions of wonder and gratitude for past experiences or invocations of guidance and protection for future travels toward the "thin places" of God. In time, both for the original pilgrims and those that follow in their footsteps, these prayers also become "thin places" as they preserve past memories and provoke future desires.

Ignatius of Loyola's "Thin Places" of God's Love

This spiritual transformation of one person's life-journey into a series of "thin places" to be visited by others lies at the heart of this collection of prayers, which emerged as part of a broader exploration the connections between Celtic and Ignatian spirituality. At the heart of Ignatius of Loyola's spiritual vision lies an awareness of the loving activity of God in all of creation and a desire to respond to this love in kind through acts of service to God, humanity and the rest of creation. In his *Spiritual Exercises*, Ignatius transforms the "thin places" of his own spiritual life-journey into a sequential collection of meditations and contemplations that shape this collection of prayer sequences.

More precisely, the organization of spiritual desires in the Ignatian exercises define the structure and content of the prayers in this book. The meditations and contemplations in Ignatius' *Spiritual Exercises* begin with a preparatory prayer asking to better understand some aspect of God's love or to help the person respond to that love. In this way, each prayer remains connected to a specific "thin place" by a holy desire but also retains its link to a larger pilgrimage of faith. So, with this in mind, the prayer sequences in this collection use new language to express Ignatius' spiritual desires but preserve the structure of those desires in the original Ignatian exercises.

Approaching the Prayer Sequences in this Book

As reminders of the graces desired from God when facing the rigors of daily life, the sequences are designed to focus on specific moments and spiritual needs. Echoing the psalms of the Bible, these prayers are written in the first person to express the individual nature of prayer but they also may be used with others in shared worship. When used in private prayer, these prayer sequences allow individuals to bring their personal desires and needs before God. However, when used in community, these prayers allow solitary voices to weave together in an expression of collective neediness before God.

Note: *This balance between individual prayer and communal worship makes it important that all members of the group using the sequence are comfortable with the graces being asked. This may require some type of communication and coordination within the group, especially if the prayer sequences are being used discreetly as specific expressions of holy desires.*

The use of the sequences by individuals requires some small preparations — the selection of the readings and the choice of music, if desired — but the communal use of these prayers requires greater coordination. The group will need to decide whether it wishes to be led in prayer or to pray as an antiphonal choir. Once that decision has been made, the leader (or one side of the chorus) should read the lines on the margin and the rest of the group respond with those lines that are indented. Similarly, the group will need to decide who will read the scriptural selection, how the psalm will be recited (i.e., together or antiphonally), and if (and how) music will be included.

Also, like the Ignatian exercises which shape the prayers in this book, the sequences are quite flexible and serve both as individual expressions of human needs and as part of a broader pilgrimage of prayer. With this in mind, the prayer sequences are organized in three thematic sections: God's love and forgiveness of sinners (Section 1), the invitation to become co-workers with Jesus (Section 2), and the redemptive ministry of the Cross and Resurrection (Section 3). So, individuals or groups need to decide whether to use the sequences in this collection as discrete prayers or in the order specified in each thematic section. Also, since the sections are progressive, individuals and groups may pray through all three thematic clusters in order.

It also is important to remember that these sequences resonate with the words of the men and women whose own devotions were gathered in the source materials used in the preparation of this collection of prayers. A delicate balance between speaking the needs of the people praying with them in the present and listening for the prayers of others from the past expressed in the readings needs to be preserved. This requires maintaining a contemplative silence around the selections that allows the individuals praying the liturgy and sequences to remain receptive to these other voices — both of the generations of different Christians and of the Triune God drawing these diverse voices into the single Body of Christ — without losing an awareness of their own needs or of their own contribution to the ongoing prayer of the Church.

Note: *Suggestions for selecting readings and music for the sequences are presented in the "Resources" section at the end of this book. Except for the readings specified when using the sequences in thematic clusters for the first time, these should be regarded as recommendations and not rules.*

Whether the sequences are used for private prayer or communal worship, whether they are used discretely or thematically, it is important for individuals or groups to review them — as well as the readings and songs to be used during them — before the formal prayer times. This will allow individuals to open their hearts so they might better express the spiritual desires encapsulated in the prayers and to make space for the special graces God will provide through these prayers. Also, to assist in making space for God to speak during the sequences, it is important to consider the role of silence in the periods of prayer — whether by creating periods of reflection within the sequence or taking time to read the prayers slowly and, perhaps, taking a breath between the prayers on the margin and those which are indented.

Remembering Your Own "Thin Places" of God's Love

Like Ignatius and the ancient Celtic saints, you will visit many different "thin places" as you engage the prayer sequences in this book. Each of these encounters will be a distinct and complete moment with God, but they also will provide you with memories and guideposts in your pilgrimage of faith. These events must be preserved since they both nourish your hope as you move toward your own "place of resurrection" and help you more easily recognize God's loving activity in your life and in the world around you. So, it is important to preserve the memory each encounter with God's love you experience.

As you begin these prayer sequences, take a moment to consider how you will record your memories of them. This may take the form of a journal or some type of notebook in which you may record your recollections. Do not be surprised if you find yourself graced by spontaneous expressions of praise — whether in songs, poems or prayers of your own. It is not unusual to become more acutely aware of God's generosity during times of prayer and hitherto unseen gifts and talents might come to the surface of your consciousness. So, embrace these graces if they are given.

Finally, after taking time with all your preparations, remember it is God who will both guide you through these prayer sequences and fulfill the holy desires you bring to them. Allow yourself to be led by God's generous graces and to be absorbed into God's surprising acts of love, recalling T. S. Eliot's admonition on pilgrimage in "Little Gidding":

> You are not here to verify,
> Instruct yourself, or inform curiosity
> Or carry report. You are here to kneel
> Where prayer has been valid.

The Prayer Sequences

From Loss to Love

1.1   O Splendour Of God's Face

---

a prayer of gratitude for the Triune God's generosity

Take a moment to quiet your spirit, becoming completely present to this time and place. Allow all other thoughts and concerns to fall away as you come into the presence of God. Then, when you are ready, begin.

O Splendour of God's face,
Bringer of glory from above,
> True light, and Fount of every grace,
> Illume my day with faith and love.

Pour on my way, O Sun Divine,
Your holy truth with rays serene,
> And let the heavenly spirit shine
> With purging fires to make me clean.

A Hymn, sung or heard (optional)

O God, I believe in you; strengthen my belief.
I trust in you; confirm my trust.
> I love you; double my love.
> I repent that I angered you,
> Increase my repentance.

I adore you as first-beginning of my life.
I desire you as my last end.
> I give thanks to you as my ever-helper.
> I call upon you as my strong-defender.

Fill you my heart with awe without despair;
With hope, without over-confidence;
> With piety without infatuation;
> And with joy without excess.

My God, consent to guide me by your wisdom;
To constrain me by your right;

To comfort me by your mercy;
And to protect me by your power.

I offer to you all my thoughts, words, deeds and sufferings.
So that from hence-forward I may think on you faithfully,
May converse of you lovingly, may labour for you devotedly,
And may suffer for you cheerfully.

A Psalm, read or recited

Holy Triune God,
Father, Son and Spirit
Under my thoughts may I God-thoughts find.
Half of my sins escape my mind.
For what I said, or did not say,
Pardon me, O Lord, I pray.

A Scriptural Selection, read aloud or quietly

O Holy God,
Father, Son and Spirit
If I were in Heaven my harp I would sound
With apostles and angels and saints all around,
Praising and thanking the Son *who is* crowned,
May the poor race of Eve for that heaven be bound!

I cry out to you, O Triune God.
Both morning and night.
Come to me, guide me,
And save me from fright,

And make me repentant
And wash me with tears,
And lead me to heaven
When spent are my years.

O Holy God,
Father, Son and Spirit
For me is many a snare designed,
To fill my mind with doubts and fears;

Far from the land of holy saints,
I dwell within my vale of tears.
Let faith, let hope, let love —
Traits far above the cold world's way —
With patience, humility, and awe,
Become my guides from day to day.

I acknowledge, the evil I have done.
From the day of my birth till the day of my death,
Through the sight of my eyes,
Through the hearing of my ears,
Through the sayings of my mouth,
Through the thoughts of my heart,
Through the touch of my hands,
Through the course of my way,
Through all I said and did not,
Through all I promised and fulfilled not,
Through all the laws and holy commandments I broke.
I ask even now absolution of you,
In the sweet name of Jesus Christ,
For fear I may have never asked it as was right,
And that I might not live to ask it again,

O Divine Majesty,
Father, Son and Spirit
May you not let my soul stray from you,
May you keep me in a good state,
May you turn me toward what is good to do,
May you protect me from dangers, small and great.
May you fill my eyes with tears of repentance,
So I may avoid the sinner's awful sentence.
May the Grace of the God for ever be with me,
And whatever my needs, may the Triune God give me.

Select one of the following options for the Lord's Prayer.

Option A

O God,
Father, Son and Spirit,

Help me pray as Jesus himself taught:
"Our Father in heaven,
hallowed be your name.
Your kingdom come.
Your will be done,
on earth as it is in heaven.
Give us this day our daily bread.
And forgive us our debts,
as we also have forgiven our debtors.
And do not bring us to the time of trial,
but rescue us from the evil one."
(Matthew 6: 9-13)
From the foes of my land,
from the foes of my faith,
From the foes who would us dissever,
O Trinity preserve me, in life, in death,
With the Sign of the Cross for ever.
For the kingdom, the power, and the glory
are yours now and for ever. Amen.

Please proceed with "I beseech the wonderful and blessed Trinity,…,"
found after Option B.

Option B

O God,
Father, Son and Spirit,
Help me pray as Jesus himself taught:
Our Father in heaven,
hallowed be your name,
your kingdom come,
your will be done,
on earth as in heaven.
Give us today our daily bread.
Forgive us our sins
as we forgive those who sin against us.
Lead us not into temptation
but deliver us from evil.
From the foes of my land,
from the foes of my faith,

From the foes who would us dissever,
   O Trinity preserve me, in life, in death,
   With the Sign of the Cross for ever.
   For the kingdom, the power, and the glory
   are yours now and for ever. Amen.

I beseech the wonderful and blessed Trinity,
God in Heaven, unsurpassed in power and might;
   Be behind me, Be on my left,
   Be before me, Be on my right!
Against each danger, God is my help;
In distress, upon the Divine Majesty I call.
   In dark times, may my God sustain me
   And lift me up again when I fall.
Lord over heaven and of earth,
The Triune God knows my offenses.
   Yet, listening to my pleadings,
   Guides me away from sinful pretenses.
Lord of all creation and the many creatures,
My God bestows on me many earthly treasures.
   Revealing love in each life and season,
   My God shares with me heavenly pleasures.
May the Holy Trinity arouse me
In moments both of joy and of strife;
   God the Father, with Mary's mighty Son,
   And the noble Spirit, bring me new life!

A Hymn, sung or heard (optional)

O Divine Majesty,
Three in one Godhead, without division.
   You are my riches, my store, my provision,
My star through the years
When troubles rend me,
   Through times of strife and tears,
   O God, defend me.

Confirm me in your love divine,
Smooth for my feet life's rugged way;
   My will with yours entwine,

Lest evil lead my steps astray.

Be with me still as guard and guide,
Keep me in holy sanctity,
    Let my firm faith on you abide,
    From fraud and error hold me free.

End this time of prayer by taking some time to bring to mind the various ways God shields you from harm or guides you through the world's tumult. Then, when you are ready, conclude by saying:

O Holy Triune God,
Father, Son and Spirit,
I place myself at the edge of your grace,
    On the floor of your house myself I place,
And to banish the sin of my heart away,
    I lower my knee to you this day.
Through life's torrents of pain may you bring me whole,
    And, O Blessed Trinity, preserve also my soul. Amen.

1.2 O Word of Might, That Springing Forth

a prayer of gratitude and commitment to Jesus

Take a moment to quiet your spirit, becoming completely present to this time and place. Allow all other thoughts and concerns to fall away as you come into the presence of God. Then, when you are ready, begin.

O Word of Might, that springing forth
From out the Father's heart, was born
        To raise my fallen state on earth,
        Bring help, and leave me not forlorn.

Illume my breast with heavenly light,
And set my soul aflame with love,
        That I, forsaking things of night,
        Shall lift my hopes to joys above.

A Hymn, sung or heard (optional)

O Lord, make me wise in the things that pass near me.
        Valiant in danger, patient in tribulation,
        And humble in going forward through the world.

May I never forget
To put heed in my prayers,
        Moderation in my ways,
        Earnestness in my cares,
        And perseverance in the things I set before me.

O Lord, Jesus the Christ,
Stir me up to keep a right conscience,
        Give me courtesy on the out-side,
        Profitable conversation, and orderly bearing.

Vouchsafe me always
To get the upper hand of my natural disposition
        By inclining to your graces,

By fulfilling your commandments,
And by working out my salvation.

Show me, Lord, the nothingness of this world,
The majesty of heaven above,
>   The shortness of time
>   And the length of eternity.

Grant me to put myself into a state of fitness for death,
To be afraid of your judgment,
>   To shun condemnation,
>   And at last to gain heaven.

A Psalm, read or recited

Holy Lord,
Under my thoughts may I God-thoughts find.
Half of my sins escape my mind.
>   For what I said, or did not say,
>   Pardon me, O Lord, I pray.

A Scriptural Selection, read aloud or quietly

O Lord, Jesus the Christ,
If I were in Heaven my harp I would sound
With apostles and angels and saints all around,
>   Praising and thanking you who is crowned above,
>   May the poor race of Eve for that heaven be bound!

Holy Lord,
In your hands I do lay my soul.
Let it not fall out of your control,
>   Countenance brighter than the sun,
>   Shield me from pain when the race is run.

The will of God be done by me,
The law of God be kept surely,
>   My evil will controlled by me,
>   My tongue in check be held securely,

Repentance timely made by me,
Your passion understood contritely,
    Each sinful crime be shunned by me,
    And my sins be mused nightly.

O Holy Lord,
    God with the Father and the Spirit,
For me is many a snare designed,
To fill my mind with doubts and fears;
    Far from the land of holy saints,
    I dwell within my vale of tears.
Let faith, let hope, let love —
Traits far above the cold world's way —
    With patience, humility, and awe,
    Become my guides from day to day.

I acknowledge, the evil I have done.
From the day of my birth till the day of my death,
    Through the sight of my eyes,
Through the hearing of my ears,
    Through the sayings of my mouth,
Through the thoughts of my heart,
    Through the touch of my hands,
Through the course of my way,
    Through all I said and did not,
Through all I promised and fulfilled not,
    Through all the laws and holy commandments I broke.
I ask even now absolution of you,
    For fear I may have never asked it as was right,
    And that I might not live to ask it again,

O Holy Lord, my King in Heaven,
May you not let my soul stray from you,
May you keep me in a good state,
    May you turn me toward what is good to do,
    May you protect me from dangers, small and great.
May you fill my eyes with tears of repentance,
    So I may avoid the sinner's awful sentence.
May the Grace of the God for ever be with me,
    And whatever my needs, may the Triune God give me.

Select one of the following options for the Lord's Prayer.

Option A

O Jesus Christ,
Lord of heaven and earth,
Help me pray as you yourself taught:
> *"Our Father in heaven,*
> *hallowed be your name.*
> *Your kingdom come.*
> *Your will be done,*
> *on earth as it is in heaven.*
> *Give us this day our daily bread.*
> *And forgive us our debts,*
> *as we also have forgiven our debtors.*
> *And do not bring us to the time of trial,*
> *but rescue us from the evil one."*
> *(Matthew 6: 9-13)*

From the foes of my land,
from the foes of my faith,
From the foes who would us dissever,
> O Lord, preserve me, in life and in death,
> With the Sign of the Cross for ever.
> *For the kingdom, the power, and the glory*
> *are yours now and for ever. Amen.*

Please proceed with "I beseech you, O Lord...," found after Option B.

Option B

O Jesus Christ,
Lord of heaven and earth,
Help me pray as you yourself taught:
> *Our Father in heaven,*
> *hallowed be your name,*
> *your kingdom come,*
> *your will be done,*
> *on earth as in heaven.*

20

Give us today our daily bread.
Forgive us our sins
as we forgive those who sin against us.
Lead us not into temptation
but deliver us from evil.
From the foes of my land,
from the foes of my faith,
From the foes who would us dissever,
O Lord, preserve me, in life and in death,
With the Sign of the Cross for ever.
For the kingdom, the power, and the glory
are yours now and for ever. Amen.

I beseech you, O Lord.
God in Heaven, unsurpassed in power and might;
Be behind me, Be on my left,
Be before me, Be on my right!
Against each danger, you are my help;
In distress, upon you I call.
In dark times, may you sustain me
And lift me up again when I fall.
Lord over heaven and of earth,
You know my offenses.
Yet, listening to my pleadings,
You guide me away from sinful pretenses.
Lord of all creation and the many creatures,
You bestow on me many earthly treasures.
Revealing love in each life and season,
You share with me heavenly pleasures.
May you arouse me
In moments both of joy and of strife;
Most holy Lord, bring me new life!

A Hymn, sung or heard (optional)

O Jesus Christ,
Lord of heaven and earth,
You are my riches, my store, my provision,
My star through the years
When troubles rend me,

Through times of strife and tears,
Sweet Jesus, defend me.

The faith that fires the holy heart,
The true believer's blessed hope,
    And perfect love, these powers impart,
    The strength with evil force to cope.

To me your tender mercy lend,
And hear the humble prayers I raise;
    In holy love my voice blend;
    Make strong my heart to sing your praise.

***End this time of prayer by taking some time to bring to mind
the various ways God shields you from harm or guides you through
the world's tumult. Then, when you are ready, conclude by saying:***

O Word of Might,
O Holy Lord, King in Heaven,
I place myself at the edge of your grace,
    On the floor of your house myself I place,
And to banish the sin of my heart away,
    I lower my knee to you this day.
Through life's torrents of pain may you bring me whole,
    And, O Lord Jesus Christ, preserve also my soul. Amen.

a sinner's prayer of remorse

Take a moment to quiet your spirit, becoming completely present to this time and place. Allow all other thoughts and concerns to fall away as you come into the presence of God. Then, when you are ready, begin.

Shamed and shaken sore with terror,
Lo! I fall before your face,
     Every grievous wrong and error
     Filling me with deep disgrace;
From the gulf deliver me;
     Cleanse me, Christ, and make me free.

I have walked in carnal pleasure,
Lived for worldly joys alone,
     Never sought your living treasure,
     Nought to please your will have done;
All my crimes in grief I see;
     Lord, be merciful to me.

A Hymn, sung or heard (optional)

Cast from the highest heights of heaven,
Far from the angels' shining state,
     Faded from glory, Lucifer,
     Falling in scorn infatuate.
Angels apostate share his fall,
Steeled with his hate and fired with pride,
     Banished from their fellows bright,
     Who in the heavenly seats abide.

Against Satan's wiles and hell's assault
Our primal parents could not stand:
     And into new abysses fell
     The leader and his horrid band:
Fierce forms, with noise of beating wings,

Too dread for sight of mortal eye,
      Who, fettered, far from human ken,
      Within their prison houses lie.

Lucifer, banished from his first estate,
The Lord cast out for evermore;
      And now his wild and rebel crew
      In upper air together soar.
Invisible lest men should gaze
On wickedness without a name,
      And, breaking every barrier down,
      Defile themselves in open shame.

A Psalm, read or recited

Holy Lord,
Under my thoughts may I God-thoughts find.
Half of my sins escape my mind.
      For what I said, or did not say,
      Pardon me, O Lord, I pray.

A Scriptural Selection, read aloud or quietly

O Lord, Jesus the Christ,
If I were in Heaven my harp I would sound
With apostles and angels and saints all around,
      Praising and thanking the Son who is crowned,
      May the poor race of Eve for that heaven be bound!

Holy Lord,
O King of heaven who did create
The man who ate of that sad tree.
      To you I cry, "Oh turn your face,
      Show heavenly grace this day to me".

From the sin of the apple, the crime of two,
Our virtues are few, our lust runs free;
      For my riotous appetite Christ alone
      From his mercy's throne can pardon me.

O Holy Lord,
>God with the Father and the Spirit,
For me is many a snare designed,
To fill my mind with doubts and fears;
>Far from the land of holy saints,
>I dwell within my vale of tears.
Let faith, let hope, let love —
Traits far above the cold world's way —
>With patience, humility, and awe,
>Become my guides from day to day.

I acknowledge, the evil I have done.
From the day of my birth till the day of my death,
>Through the sight of my eyes,
Through the hearing of my ears,
>Through the sayings of my mouth,
Through the thoughts of my heart,
>Through the touch of my hands,
Through the course of my way,
>Through all I said and did not,
Through all I promised and fulfilled not,
>Through all the laws and holy commandments I broke.
I ask even now absolution of you,
>For fear I may have never asked it as was right,
>And that I might not live to ask it again,

O Holy Lord, my King in Heaven,
May you not let my soul stray from you,
May you keep me in a good state,
>May you turn me toward what is good to do,
>May you protect me from dangers, small and great.
May you fill my eyes with tears of repentance,
>So I may avoid the sinner's awful sentence.
May the Grace of the God for ever be with me,
>And whatever my needs, may the Triune God give me.

Select one of the following options for the Lord's Prayer.

Option A

O Jesus Christ,
Lord of heaven and earth,
Help me pray as you yourself taught:
>"*Our Father in heaven,*
>*hallowed be your name.*
>*Your kingdom come.*
>*Your will be done,*
>*on earth as it is in heaven.*
>*Give us this day our daily bread.*
>*And forgive us our debts,*
>*as we also have forgiven our debtors.*
>*And do not bring us to the time of trial,*
>*but rescue us from the evil one."*
>*(Matthew 6: 9-13)*

From the foes of my land,
from the foes of my faith,
From the foes who would us dissever,
>O Lord, preserve me, in life and in death,
>With the Sign of the Cross for ever.
>*For the kingdom, the power, and the glory*
>*are yours now and for ever. Amen.*

Please proceed with "I beseech you, O Lord...," found after Option B.

Option B

O Jesus Christ,
Lord of heaven and earth,
Help me pray as you yourself taught:
>*Our Father in heaven,*
>*hallowed be your name,*
>*your kingdom come,*
>*your will be done,*
>*on earth as in heaven.*
>*Give us today our daily bread.*
>*Forgive us our sins*
>*as we forgive those who sin against us.*
>*Lead us not into temptation*
>*but deliver us from evil.*

From the foes of my land,
from the foes of my faith,
From the foes who would us dissever,
O Lord, preserve me, in life and in death,
With the Sign of the Cross for ever.
For the kingdom, the power, and the glory
are yours now and for ever. Amen.

I beseech you, O Lord.
God in Heaven, unsurpassed in power and might;
Be behind me, Be on my left,
Be before me, Be on my right!
Against each danger, you are my help;
In distress, upon you I call.
In dark times, may you sustain me
And lift me up again when I fall.
Lord over heaven and of earth,
You know my offenses.
Yet, listening to my pleadings,
You guide me away from sinful pretenses.
Lord of all creation and the many creatures,
You bestow on me many earthly treasures.
Revealing love in each life and season,
You share with me heavenly pleasures.
May you arouse me
In moments both of joy and of strife;
Most holy Lord, bring me new life!

A Hymn, sung or heard (optional)

O Jesus Christ,
Lord of heaven and earth,
You are my riches, my store, my provision,
My star through the years
When troubles rend me,
Through times of strife and tears,
Sweet Jesus, defend me.

Long in feasting and in riot,
In deceptions vile and vain,

I have walked with heart unquiet,
    Fouled my soul with sinful stain ;
From the depths I cry to you.
    Lord, be merciful to me.

Jesus, Maker and Defender,
Sweet Redeemer of mankind,
    Hear me in your mercy tender,
    Let my soul your pardon find ;
From my woes deliver me ;
    Cleanse and raise me unto you.

End this time of prayer by taking some time to bring to mind the various ways God shields you from harm or guides you through the world's tumult. Then, when you are ready, conclude by saying:

O Holy Lord, King in Heaven,
I place myself at the edge of your grace,
    On the floor of your house myself I place,
And to banish the sin of my heart away,
    I lower my knee to you this day.
Through life's torrents of pain may you bring me whole,
    And, O Lord Jesus Christ, preserve also my soul. Amen.

a prayer for redemption from sin

Take a moment to quiet your spirit, becoming completely present to this time and place. Allow all other thoughts and concerns to fall away as you come into the presence of God. Then, when you are ready, begin.

I call on you to save me,
From grovelling deeds of shame;
        O make me yours by grace divine,
        To love and bless your name.

Drive from my heart all darkness,
All evil from my mind;
        Forever be my joy in you,
        O Saviour of mankind.

A Hymn, sung or heard (optional)

Sweet Jesus, help the foolish sinner
Who strays, with none to guard.
        He rises up in the morning's light
        But thinks not on his God.

Prayer and the blessed word of God
He never hears them read,
        And when he leaves this world at last,
        Ah, where shall be his bed?

You Christians, do you hear me?
Be thinking of the Death.
        The night to it is as the day
        To sweep away your breath.

And he who mocked at penitence
When he was on the world,
        To frost and cold outside the fold

Too soon shall he be hurled.

When the soul shall go up to the gate of heaven
That has made not its peace with the Son of God,
      The angels shall cry and the saints shall say
      you did not, soul, foresee this day,
      When alive upon earth's green sod.

A Psalm, read or recited

Holy Lord,
Under my thoughts may I God-thoughts find.
Half of my sins escape my mind.
      For what I said, or did not say,
      Pardon me, O Lord, I pray.

A Scriptural Selection, read aloud or quietly

O Lord, Jesus the Christ,
If I were in Heaven my harp I would sound
With apostles and angels and saints all around,
      Praising and thanking the Son who is crowned,
      May the poor race of Eve for that heaven be bound!

Holy Lord,
May you show mercy upon me with your grace.
      Showing forgiveness and mercy to my soul.
May you put nothing in my heart
      That may take my share of the eternal glory of the heavens
from me.
May you saye me from the showers of calamity,
      And from the diseases of the year.
May you nurture in me, in life and in health,
      The love of God and of my neighbours.

O Holy Lord,
      God with the Father and the Spirit,
For me is many a snare designed,
To fill my mind with doubts and fears;
      Far from the land of holy saints,

I dwell within my vale of tears.
Let faith, let hope, let love —
Traits far above the cold world's way —
    With patience, humility, and awe,
    Become my guides from day to day.

I acknowledge, the evil I have done.
From the day of my birth till the day of my death,
    Through the sight of my eyes,
Through the hearing of my ears,
    Through the sayings of my mouth,
Through the thoughts of my heart,
    Through the touch of my hands,
Through the course of my way,
    Through all I said and did not,
Through all I promised and fulfilled not,
    Through all the laws and holy commandments I broke.
I ask even now absolution of you,
    For fear I may have never asked it as was right,
    And that I might not live to ask it again,

O Holy Lord, my King in Heaven,
May you not let my soul stray from you,
May you keep me in a good state,
    May you turn me toward what is good to do,
    May you protect me from dangers, small and great.
May you fill my eyes with tears of repentance,
    So I may avoid the sinner's awful sentence.
May the Grace of the God for ever be with me,
    And whatever my needs, may the Triune God give me.

Select one of the following options for the Lord's Prayer.

Option A

O Jesus Christ,
Lord of heaven and earth,
Help me pray as you yourself taught:
    "Our Father in heaven,
    hallowed be your name.

Your kingdom come.
Your will be done,
on earth as it is in heaven.
Give us this day our daily bread.
And forgive us our debts,
as we also have forgiven our debtors.
And do not bring us to the time of trial,
but rescue us from the evil one."
(Matthew 6: 9-13)

From the foes of my land,
from the foes of my faith,
From the foes who would us dissever,
    O Lord, preserve me, in life and in death,
    With the Sign of the Cross for ever.
    For the kingdom, the power, and the glory
    are yours now and for ever. Amen.

Please proceed with "I beseech you, O Lord...," found after Option B.

Option B

O Jesus Christ,
Lord of heaven and earth,
Help me pray as you yourself taught:
    Our Father in heaven,
    hallowed be your name,
    your kingdom come,
    your will be done,
    on earth as in heaven.
    Give us today our daily bread.
    Forgive us our sins
    as we forgive those who sin against us.
    Lead us not into temptation
    but deliver us from evil.

From the foes of my land,
from the foes of my faith,
From the foes who would us dissever,
    O Lord, preserve me, in life and in death,
    With the Sign of the Cross for ever.

For the kingdom, the power, and the glory
are yours now and for ever. Amen.

I beseech you, O Lord.
God in Heaven, unsurpassed in power and might;
      Be behind me, Be on my left,
      Be before me, Be on my right!
Against each danger, you are my help;
In distress, upon you I call.
      In dark times, may you sustain me
      And lift me up again when I fall.
Lord over heaven and of earth,
You know my offenses.
      Yet, listening to my pleadings,
      You guide me away from sinful pretenses.
Lord of all creation and the many creatures,
You bestow on me many earthly treasures.
      Revealing love in each life and season,
      You share with me heavenly pleasures.
May you arouse me
In moments both of joy and of strife;
      Most holy Lord, bring me new life!

A Hymn, sung or heard (optional)

O Jesus Christ,
      Lord of heaven and earth,
      You are my riches, my store, my provision,
My star through the years
When troubles rend me,
      Through times of strife and tears,
      Sweet Jesus, defend me.

Lo, though my heart is evil,
Though strong the tempter's power,
      I dare to raise my voice in praise,
      And seek you every hour.

Drive from my heart all darkness,
All evil from my mind;

Forever be my joy in you,
O Saviour of mankind.

End this time of prayer by taking some time to bring to mind the various ways God shields you from harm or guides you through the world's tumult. Then, when you are ready, conclude by saying:

O Holy Lord, King in Heaven,
I place myself at the edge of your grace,
    On the floor of your house myself I place,
And to banish the sin of my heart away,
    I lower my knee to you this day.
Through life's torrents of pain may you bring me whole,
    And, O Lord Jesus Christ, preserve also my soul. Amen.

1.5   Loving Jesus, Hear Me Calling

a sinner's plea for mercy and assistance

Take a moment to quiet your spirit, becoming completely present to this time and place. Allow all other thoughts and concerns to fall away as you come into the presence of God. Then, when you are ready, begin.

Loving Jesus, hear me calling,
Me, a sinner, poor and weak;
>Lo, I stretch mine arms to clasp you,
>And your tender solace seek,
Lest mine enemies against me
>Rise, their deeds of woe to wreak.

They that seek my soul in envy,
That would lead me from your throne,
>Be the wicked will their ruin,
>In destruction let them groan;
But, my Saviour, hear my pleading,
>Raise me, leave me not alone.

A Hymn, sung or heard (optional)

At the first sound of the trumpet's blast
The heavens shall be overcast.
>Each poor feeble soul must rise,
>And each cold body likewise.

Then some shall be whiter
Than the snow of December,
>And some shall be blacker
>Than the smith's burnt ember.

Then Christ shall stand, when all are sent,
>Delivering His Judgment.

Christ shall speak unto all assembled

"Listen to me, all you Good and Blest,
Come hither and stand upon
My right hand until I bring you to My Father's rest."

> Then Christ shall speak unto all again,
> "Depart from me, all you Bad and Curst,
> You are given to yonder foul black devils
> To work henceforth on you their worst."

A Psalm, read or recited

Holy Lord,
Under my thoughts may I God-thoughts find.
Half of my sins escape my mind.
> For what I said, or did not say,
> Pardon me, O Lord, I pray.

A Scriptural Selection, read aloud or quietly

O Lord, Jesus the Christ,
If I were in Heaven my harp I would sound
With apostles and angels and saints all around,
> Praising and thanking the Son who is crowned,
> May the poor race of Eve for that heaven be bound!

Holy Lord,
Help this foolish sinner,
I always go astray,
> I rise up in the morning
> But pray not with the day.
God I has long forsaken —
Forgotten how to pray,
> Where shall I go when Death shall come
> And I leave the world in disarray.

O Holy Lord,
> God with the Father and the Spirit,
For me is many a snare designed,
To fill my mind with doubts and fears;
> Far from the land of holy saints,

I dwell within my vale of tears.
Let faith, let hope, let love —
Traits far above the cold world's way —
    With patience, humility, and awe,
    Become my guides from day to day.

I acknowledge, the evil I have done.
From the day of my birth till the day of my death,
    Through the sight of my eyes,
Through the hearing of my ears,
    Through the sayings of my mouth,
Through the thoughts of my heart,
    Through the touch of my hands,
Through the course of my way,
    Through all I said and did not,
Through all I promised and fulfilled not,
    Through all the laws and holy commandments I broke.
I ask even now absolution of you,
    For fear I may have never asked it as was right,
    And that I might not live to ask it again,

O Holy Lord, my King in Heaven,
May you not let my soul stray from you,
May you keep me in a good state,
    May you turn me toward what is good to do,
    May you protect me from dangers, small and great.
May you fill my eyes with tears of repentance,
    So I may avoid the sinner's awful sentence.
May the Grace of the God for ever be with me,
    And whatever my needs, may the Triune God give me.

Select one of the following options for the Lord's Prayer.

Option A

O Jesus Christ,
Lord of heaven and earth,
Help me pray as you yourself taught:
    "Our Father in heaven,
    hallowed be your name.

Your kingdom come.
Your will be done,
on earth as it is in heaven.
Give us this day our daily bread.
And forgive us our debts,
as we also have forgiven our debtors.
And do not bring us to the time of trial,
but rescue us from the evil one. "
(Matthew 6: 9-13)
From the foes of my land,
from the foes of my faith,
From the foes who would us dissever,
O Lord, preserve me, in life and in death,
With the Sign of the Cross for ever.
For the kingdom, the power, and the glory
are yours now and for ever. Amen.

Please proceed with "I beseech you, O Lord...," found after Option B.

Option B

O Jesus Christ,
Lord of heaven and earth,
Help me pray as you yourself taught:
Our Father in heaven,
hallowed be your name,
your kingdom come,
your will be done,
on earth as in heaven.
Give us today our daily bread.
Forgive us our sins
as we forgive those who sin against us.
Lead us not into temptation
but deliver us from evil.
From the foes of my land,
from the foes of my faith,
From the foes who would us dissever,
O Lord, preserve me, in life and in death,
With the Sign of the Cross for ever.

For the kingdom, the power, and the glory
are yours now and for ever. Amen.

I beseech you, O Lord.
God in Heaven, unsurpassed in power and might;
  Be behind me, Be on my left,
  Be before me, Be on my right!
Against each danger, you are my help;
In distress, upon you I call.
  In dark times, may you sustain me
  And lift me up again when I fall.
Lord over heaven and of earth,
You know my offenses.
  Yet, listening to my pleadings,
  You guide me away from sinful pretenses.
Lord of all creation and the many creatures,
You bestow on me many earthly treasures.
  Revealing love in each life and season,
  You share with me heavenly pleasures.
May you arouse me
In moments both of joy and of strife;
  Most holy Lord, bring me new life!

A Hymn, sung or heard (optional)

O Jesus Christ,
  Lord of heaven and earth,
  You are my riches, my store, my provision,
My star through the years
When troubles rend me,
  Through times of strife and tears,
  Sweet Jesus, defend me.

Be your cross my royal symbol,
Be its holy sign my guard;
  While against the foe, unwearied,
  I shall still keep watch and ward;
Till the powers of darkness, conquered,
  Shall adore your throne, O Lord.

Son of God, the everliving,
Tender Saviour, hear and heed,
      See me, Lord of angels, weeping,
      Crying out to you in need;
Grant me mercy, grant forgiveness,
      Virtue grant in word and deed.

End this time of prayer by taking some time to bring to mind the various ways God shields you from harm or guides you through the world's tumult. Then, when you are ready, conclude by saying:

O Holy Lord, King in Heaven,
I place myself at the edge of your grace,
      On the floor of your house myself I place,
And to banish the sin of my heart away,
      I lower my knee to you this day.
Through life's torrents of pain may you bring me whole,
     And, O Lord Jesus Christ, preserve also my soul. Amen.

a prayer of humble contrition

Take a moment to quiet your spirit, becoming completely present to this time and place. Allow all other thoughts and concerns to fall away as you come into the presence of God. Then, when you are ready, begin.

I am not worthy, O God, mine eyes
To turn unto your starry skies;
> But bowed in sin, with moans and sighs,
> I beg you, hear me.

My duty I have left undone,
Nor sought I crime or shame to shun,
> My feet in sinful paths have run,
> Sweet Christ, be near me.

A Hymn, sung or heard (optional)

My God, give me strength
So that I may make expiation for my misdeeds,
> So that I may win victory over my temptations,
> So that I may right my strong evil-inclinations,
And so that I may practise the virtues
> That are suitable to my state of life.

Fill my heart with affection for your goodness,
With hatred of my faults, with love for my neighbours,
> And with contempt for the world.
> That I may remember, O God,
To be submissive to my superiors,
To be at one with my inferiors,
> Faithful to my friends
> And charitable to my enemies.

Aid me to gain a victory
Over fleshly desires by piety,

Over covetousness by alms-giving,
Over passion by mildness,
And over hypocrisy by earnestness.

A Psalm, read or recited

Holy Triune God,
  Father, Son and Spirit
Under my thoughts may I God-thoughts find.
Half of my sins escape my mind.
  For what I said, or did not say,
  Pardon me, O Lord, I pray.

A Scriptural Selection, read aloud or quietly

O Holy God,
  Father, Son and Spirit
If I were in Heaven my harp I would sound
With apostles and angels and saints all around,
  Praising and thanking the Son who is crowned,
  May the poor race of Eve for that heaven be bound!

Holy Triune God,
Weakly I go from the load within,
Deeply repenting with woe my sin.
  I acknowledge faith in my God all my days
  With love from my heart and with hope always,

From the foot of your cross I call to you
Jesus, Lord, bow down to me.
  For I stand in the faith of my God to-day,
  Put love in my heart and hope away.

O Holy God,
  Father, Son and Spirit
For me is many a snare designed,
To fill my mind with doubts and fears;
  Far from the land of holy saints,
  I dwell within my vale of tears.
Let faith, let hope, let love —

Traits far above the cold world's way —
> With patience, humility, and awe,
> Become my guides from day to day.

I acknowledge, the evil I have done.
From the day of my birth till the day of my death,
> Through the sight of my eyes,
Through the hearing of my ears,
> Through the sayings of my mouth,
Through the thoughts of my heart,
> Through the touch of my hands,
Through the course of my way,
> Through all I said and did not,
Through all I promised and fulfilled not,
> Through all the laws and holy commandments I broke.
I ask even now absolution of you,
In the sweet name of Jesus Christ,
> For fear I may have never asked it as was right,
> And that I might not live to ask it again,

O Divine Majesty,
> Father, Son and Spirit
May you not let my soul stray from you,
May you keep me in a good state,
> May you turn me toward what is good to do,
> May you protect me from dangers, small and great.
May you fill my eyes with tears of repentance,
> So I may avoid the sinner's awful sentence.
May the Grace of the God for ever be with me,
> And whatever my needs, may the Triune God give me.

Select one of the following options for the Lord's Prayer.

Option A

O God,
Father, Son and Spirit,
help me pray as Jesus himself taught:
> *"Our Father in heaven,*
> *hallowed be your name.*

Your kingdom come.
Your will be done,
on earth as it is in heaven.
Give us this day our daily bread.
And forgive us our debts,
as we also have forgiven our debtors.
And do not bring us to the time of trial,
but rescue us from the evil one."
(Matthew 6: 9-13)

From the foes of my land,
from the foes of my faith,
From the foes who would us dissever,
> O Trinity preserve me, in life, in death,
> With the Sign of the Cross for ever.
> *For the kingdom, the power, and the glory*
> *are yours now and for ever. Amen.*

Please proceed with "I beseech the wonderful and blessed Trinity,...,"
found after Option B.

Option B

O God,
Father, Son and Spirit,
help me pray as Jesus himself taught:
> *Our Father in heaven,*
> *hallowed be your name,*
> *your kingdom come,*
> *your will be done,*
> *on earth as in heaven.*
> *Give us today our daily bread.*
> *Forgive us our sins*
> *as we forgive those who sin against us.*
> *Lead us not into temptation*
> *but deliver us from evil.*

From the foes of my land,
from the foes of my faith,
From the foes who would us dissever,
> O Trinity preserve me, in life, in death,
> With the Sign of the Cross for ever.

For the kingdom, the power, and the glory
are yours now and for ever. Amen.

I beseech the wonderful and blessed Trinity,
God in Heaven, unsurpassed in power and might;
  Be behind me, Be on my left,
  Be before me, Be on my right!
Against each danger, God is my help;
In distress, upon the Divine Majesty I call.
  In dark times, may my God sustain me
  And lift me up again when I fall.
Lord over heaven and of earth,
The Triune God knows my offenses.
  Yet, listening to my pleadings,
  Guides me away from sinful pretenses.
Lord of all creation and the many creatures,
My God bestows on me many earthly treasures.
  Revealing love in each life and season,
  My God shares with me heavenly pleasures.
May the Holy Trinity arouse me
In moments both of joy and of strife;
  God the Father, with Mary's mighty Son,
  And the noble Spirit, bring me new life!

A Hymn, sung or heard (optional)

O Divine Majesty,
Three in one Godhead, without division.
  You are my riches, my store, my provision,
My star through the years
When troubles rend me,
  Through times of strife and tears,
  O God, defend me.

Fill my soul with grief sincere,
With sorrow deep for my offence;
  Let the tear moisten my pillow;
  Hear me and grant me defense.

For all my many crimes, O God,

Toward the pains of hell I sadly plod;
    But you know my repentance,
    And spare the painful sentence.

End this time of prayer by taking some time to bring to mind the various ways God shields you from harm or guides you through the world's tumult. Then, when you are ready, conclude by saying:

O Holy Triune God,
Father, Son and Spirit,
I place myself at the edge of your grace,
    On the floor of your house myself I place,
And to banish the sin of my heart away,
    I lower my knee to you this day.
Through life's torrents of pain may you bring me whole,
    And, O Blessed Trinity, preserve also my soul. Amen.

a redeemed sinner's plea for divine aid

Take a moment to quiet your spirit, becoming completely present to this time and place. Allow all other thoughts and concerns to fall away as you come into the presence of God. Then, when you are ready, begin.

Redeemer, sole-begotten Son,
With Father and Spirit, three in one,
     You are my hope; as ages run
     Be yours all glory.

If in the balance you should weigh
My crimes, there were nor hope nor stay,
     But Lord, your clemency I pray,
     To grace restore me.

A Hymn, sung or heard (optional)

The hope of my soul is in your promise,
My homage receive of me, though late:
     Your mercy is greater than my defiance,
     So I before you lie myself prostrate.

Yours is my life and Yours my death,
God of all breath, my pride is o'er!
     One glance from you were all my wealth,
     My hope, my health, for evermore!

O you who makes the dead to live,
Who didst forgive the Thief his scorn,
     Hear now, as then, a sinner's sigh,
     The bitter cry of me forlorn.

O pierced in foot and hand and side,
crucified for hearts that burn,
     I reach to you, oh reach to me,

I ne'er again from you shall turn.

O King of kings, O King of worlds,
O King who was, and is to be,
> Forgive, O King, with Father and Spirit my sins,
> Receive our prayer, and comfort me.

A Psalm, read or recited

Holy Lord,
Under my thoughts may I God-thoughts find.
Half of my sins escape my mind.
> For what I said, or did not say,
> Pardon me, O Lord, I pray.

A Scriptural Selection, read aloud or quietly

O Lord, Jesus the Christ,
If I were in Heaven my harp I would sound
With apostles and angels and saints all around,
> Praising and thanking the Son who is crowned,
> May the poor race of Eve for that heaven be bound!

Holy Lord,
Heaven may I gain,
In the well of the grace of confession
> My words, my deeds,
> And my omissions.

Help for me, friends for me, help and God's graces,
Help I am asking in all bad places,
> Jesus — with Father and Spirit — I pray
> Drive each evil thought away.

Be with me 'til break of day,
In my sleep and on my way.
> When the hour of hours shall sound
> Jesus be within me found.

O Holy Lord,

God with the Father and the Spirit,
For me is many a snare designed,
To fill my mind with doubts and fears;
    Far from the land of holy saints,
    I dwell within my vale of tears.
Let faith, let hope, let love —
Traits far above the cold world's way —
    With patience, humility, and awe,
    Become my guides from day to day.

I acknowledge, the evil I have done.
From the day of my birth till the day of my death,
    Through the sight of my eyes,
Through the hearing of my ears,
    Through the sayings of my mouth,
Through the thoughts of my heart,
    Through the touch of my hands,
Through the course of my way,
    Through all I said and did not,
Through all I promised and fulfilled not,
    Through all the laws and holy commandments I broke.
I ask even now absolution of you,
    For fear I may have never asked it as was right,
    And that I might not live to ask it again,

O Holy Lord, my King in Heaven,
May you not let my soul stray from you,
May you keep me in a good state,
    May you turn me toward what is good to do,
    May you protect me from dangers, small and great.
May you fill my eyes with tears of repentance,
    So I may avoid the sinner's awful sentence.
May the Grace of the God for ever be with me,
    And whatever my needs, may the Triune God give me.

Select one of the following options for the Lord's Prayer.

Option A

O Jesus Christ,

Lord of heaven and earth,
Help me pray as you yourself taught:
"Our Father in heaven,
hallowed be your name.
Your kingdom come.
Your will be done,
on earth as it is in heaven.
Give us this day our daily bread.
And forgive us our debts,
as we also have forgiven our debtors.
And do not bring us to the time of trial,
but rescue us from the evil one."
(Matthew 6: 9-13)
From the foes of my land,
from the foes of my faith,
From the foes who would us dissever,
O Lord, preserve me, in life and in death,
With the Sign of the Cross for ever.
For the kingdom, the power, and the glory
are yours now and for ever. Amen.

Please proceed with "I beseech you, O Lord...," found after Option B.

Option B

O Jesus Christ,
Lord of heaven and earth,
Help me pray as you yourself taught:
Our Father in heaven,
hallowed be your name,
your kingdom come,
your will be done,
on earth as in heaven.
Give us today our daily bread.
Forgive us our sins
as we forgive those who sin against us.
Lead us not into temptation
but deliver us from evil.
From the foes of my land,

50

from the foes of my faith,
From the foes who would us dissever,
>   O Lord, preserve me, in life and in death,
>   With the Sign of the Cross for ever.
>   *For the kingdom, the power, and the glory*
>   *are yours now and for ever. Amen.*

I beseech you, O Lord.
God in Heaven, unsurpassed in power and might;
>   Be behind me, Be on my left,
>   Be before me, Be on my right!
Against each danger, you are my help;
In distress, upon you I call.
>   In dark times, may you sustain me
>   And lift me up again when I fall.
Lord over heaven and of earth,
You know my offenses.
>   Yet, listening to my pleadings,
>   You guide me away from sinful pretenses.
Lord of all creation and the many creatures,
You bestow on me many earthly treasures.
>   Revealing love in each life and season,
>   You share with me heavenly pleasures.
May you arouse me
In moments both of joy and of strife;
>   Most holy Lord, bring me new life!

A Hymn, sung or heard (optional)

O Jesus Christ,
>   Lord of heaven and earth,
>   You are my riches, my store, my provision,
My star through the years
When troubles rend me,
>   Through times of strife and tears,
>   Sweet Jesus, defend me.

Creator of the heavenly light,
you gave the stars their certain way,
>   Fixing the moon to shine at night,

The fiery sun to glow by day.

Lord, let me flee each evil thing
Whereto the wicked will declines,
Let all my words and actions bring
My soul to where your glory shines.

End this time of prayer by taking some time to bring to mind the various ways God shields you from harm or guides you through the world's tumult. Then, when you are ready, conclude by saying:

O Holy Lord, King in Heaven,
I place myself at the edge of your grace,
On the floor of your house myself I place,
And to banish the sin of my heart away,
I lower my knee to you this day.
Through life's torrents of pain may you bring me whole,
And, O Lord Jesus Christ, preserve also my soul. Amen.

1.8   Holy God, Let My Tongue Be Free From Blame

a loved sinner's prayer for continued aid

Take a moment to quiet your spirit, becoming completely present to this time and place. Allow all other thoughts and concerns to fall away as you come into the presence of God. Then, when you are ready, begin.

Holy God, let my tongue be free from blame,
Nor utter words of guilt or strife;
      Lift up my eyes from deeds of shame,
      And all the vanities of life.

My heart be purged and purified
That nought of evil shall remain;
      From worldly vice and fleshly pride
      My soul by temperance restrain.

A Hymn, sung or heard (optional)

May the grace of the Holy Ghost be gained by me,
And true Faith be kept unstained by me,
      While I follow the path of the saints, endeavouring
      To walk in the temple of Christ unwavering.

Bridling the tongue so prone to mutiny,
Shunning drunkenness, shunning gluttony,
      Never to evil again inclining me,
      Seeking repentance made in time by me.

Never forsaking the rule of abstinence,
Plucking away the evil plants in me,
      Always forgiving earthly enmities,
      Purging clean my guilty conscience.

The goods of other men never envying,
Never wantonly making enemies,
      Fighting the foe of the soul for victory,

Living for ever a life of sanctity.

As my own, my friend's fame, cherishing,
God's commandments obey in everything,
      Oaths of anger for ever abandoning,
      Besmirching no one, no one blackening.

A Psalm, read or recited

Holy Triune God,
      Father, Son and Spirit
Under my thoughts may I God-thoughts find.
Half of my sins escape my mind.
      For what I said, or did not say,
      Pardon me, O Lord, I pray.

A Scriptural Selection, read aloud or quietly

O Holy God,
      Father, Son and Spirit
If I were in Heaven my harp I would sound
With apostles and angels and saints all around,
      Praising and thanking the Son who is crowned,
      May the poor race of Eve for that heaven be bound!

Holy Triune God,
May speak I the praise of the truth, not slumbering,
The end of the whole, each day remembering,
      Helping the poor and those in wretchedness,
      Musing on Christ and on His blessedness.

Striving to reach the heaven's holiness.
Paying all debts in peace and lowliness,
      Blessings of God and of men still nerving me,
      Help of apostles and saints preserving me.

O Holy God,
      Father, Son and Spirit
For me is many a snare designed,
To fill my mind with doubts and fears;

Far from the land of holy saints,
I dwell within my vale of tears.
Let faith, let hope, let love —
Traits far above the cold world's way —
With patience, humility, and awe,
Become my guides from day to day.

I acknowledge, the evil I have done.
From the day of my birth till the day of my death,
Through the sight of my eyes,
Through the hearing of my ears,
Through the sayings of my mouth,
Through the thoughts of my heart,
Through the touch of my hands,
Through the course of my way,
Through all I said and did not,
Through all I promised and fulfilled not,
Through all the laws and holy commandments I broke.
I ask even now absolution of you,
In the sweet name of Jesus Christ,
For fear I may have never asked it as was right,
And that I might not live to ask it again,

O Divine Majesty,
Father, Son and Spirit
May you not let my soul stray from you,
May you keep me in a good state,
May you turn me toward what is good to do,
May you protect me from dangers, small and great.
May you fill my eyes with tears of repentance,
So I may avoid the sinner's awful sentence.
May the Grace of the God for ever be with me,
And whatever my needs, may the Triune God give me.

Select one of the following options for the Lord's Prayer.

Option A

O God,
Father, Son and Spirit,

help me pray as Jesus himself taught:
"Our Father in heaven,
hallowed be your name.
Your kingdom come.
Your will be done,
on earth as it is in heaven.
Give us this day our daily bread.
And forgive us our debts,
as we also have forgiven our debtors.
And do not bring us to the time of trial,
but rescue us from the evil one."
(Matthew 6: 9-13)
From the foes of my land,
from the foes of my faith,
From the foes who would us dissever,
O Trinity preserve me, in life, in death,
With the Sign of the Cross for ever.
For the kingdom, the power, and the glory
are yours now and for ever. Amen.

Please proceed with "I beseech the wonderful and blessed Trinity,…,"
found after Option B.

Option B

O God,
Father, Son and Spirit,
help me pray as Jesus himself taught:
Our Father in heaven,
hallowed be your name,
your kingdom come,
your will be done,
on earth as in heaven.
Give us today our daily bread.
Forgive us our sins
as we forgive those who sin against us.
Lead us not into temptation
but deliver us from evil.
From the foes of my land,
from the foes of my faith,

56

From the foes who would us dissever,
>   O Trinity preserve me, in life, in death,
>   With the Sign of the Cross for ever.
>   *For the kingdom, the power, and the glory*
>   *are yours now and for ever. Amen.*

I beseech the wonderful and blessed Trinity,
God in Heaven, unsurpassed in power and might;
>   Be behind me, Be on my left,
>   Be before me, Be on my right!
Against each danger, God is my help;
In distress, upon the Divine Majesty I call.
>   In dark times, may my God sustain me
>   And lift me up again when I fall.
Lord over heaven and of earth,
The Triune God knows my offenses.
>   Yet, listening to my pleadings,
>   Guides me away from sinful pretenses.
Lord of all creation and the many creatures,
My God bestows on me many earthly treasures.
>   Revealing love in each life and season,
>   My God shares with me heavenly pleasures.
May the Holy Trinity arouse me
In moments both of joy and of strife;
>   God the Father, with Mary's mighty Son,
>   And the noble Spirit, bring me new life!

A Hymn, sung or heard (optional)

O Divine Majesty,
Three in one Godhead, without division.
>   You are my riches, my store, my provision,
My star through the years
When troubles rend me,
>   Through times of strife and tears,
>   O God, defend me.

So help me, O God, no evil do,
'Til fades in dusk the sunset flame,
That I unstained may come to you

57

And sing the glories of your name.

Eternal Triune Deity, your word
Made all the spheres that roll above,
   You are the everlasting Lord,
   The fount of everlasting love.

   End this time of prayer by taking some time to bring to mind
the various ways God shields you from harm or guides you through
the world's tumult. Then, when you are ready, conclude by saying:

O Holy Triune God,
Father, Son and Spirit,
I place myself at the edge of your grace,
   On the floor of your house myself I place,
And to banish the sin of my heart away,
   I lower my knee to you this day.
Through life's torrents of pain may you bring me whole,
  And, O Blessed Trinity, preserve also my soul. Amen.

1.9   Jesus, My Love, My Saviour

a loved sinner's prayer of praise and service

Take a moment to quiet your spirit, becoming completely present to this time and place. Allow all other thoughts and concerns to fall away as you come into the presence of God. Then, when you are ready, begin.

Jesus, my love, my Saviour,
The joy of every heart,
    You bring light unto my night,
    For light itself you impart.

The night of sin is broken,
The power of hell o'erthrown,
    The heavenly door made wide once more
    By you, most Holy One.

A Hymn, sung or heard (optional)

May the grace of the Holy Ghost be gained by me,
And the true Faith be kept unstained by me,
    While I follow the path of the saints, endeavouring
    To walk in the temple of Christ unwavering.

And may I seek the eternal Trinity
Trusting in Christ and in Christ's divinity,
    Helping the poor and relieving them
    Walking with God and receiving them.

Devils that tempt me, still repelling them.
All my faults to Heaven confessing them.
    Fighting with all that wounds, with energy,
    Ceasing from lies and evil calumny.

Let me not mix with strife and devilry,
Fall I to prayer instead of revelry,
    Thanking the Lord for all his generosity

Throwing aside my evil ways from me.

My life disorderly now amending it;
My evil will no more defending it;
      All sorts of sin avoiding carefully,
      In friendship with God rejoicing prayerful'y.

A Psalm, read or recited

Holy Lord,
Under my thoughts may I God-thoughts find.
Half of my sins escape my mind.
      For what I said, or did not say,
      Pardon me, O Lord, I pray.

A Scriptural Selection, read aloud or quietly

O Lord, Jesus the Christ,
If I were in Heaven my harp I would sound
With apostles and angels and saints all around,
      Praising and thanking the Son who is crowned,
      May the poor race of Eve for that heaven be bound!

Holy Lord,
The law of God may I perform
The Commandments of God may I keep,
      The glory of the Heavens may I see,
      And the sweet music of the angels may I hear.

Word of the everlasting Father,
Seal me with faith, with love inspire:
      Confirm my hope, O Holy One,
      True God and sole-begotten Son.

O Holy Lord,
      God with the Father and the Spirit,
For me is many a snare designed,
To fill my mind with doubts and fears;
      Far from the land of holy saints,
      I dwell within my vale of tears.

Let faith, let hope, let love —
Traits far above the cold world's way —
    With patience, humility, and awe,
    Become my guides from day to day.

I acknowledge, the evil I have done.
From the day of my birth till the day of my death,
    Through the sight of my eyes,
Through the hearing of my ears,
    Through the sayings of my mouth,
Through the thoughts of my heart,
    Through the touch of my hands,
Through the course of my way,
    Through all I said and did not,
Through all I promised and fulfilled not,
    Through all the laws and holy commandments I broke.
I ask even now absolution of you,
    For fear I may have never asked it as was right,
    And that I might not live to ask it again,

O Holy Lord, my King in Heaven,
May you not let my soul stray from you,
May you keep me in a good state,
    May you turn me toward what is good to do,
    May you protect me from dangers, small and great.
May you fill my eyes with tears of repentance,
    So I may avoid the sinner's awful sentence.
May the Grace of the God for ever be with me,
    And whatever my needs, may the Triune God give me.

Select one of the following options for the Lord's Prayer.

Option A

O Jesus Christ,
Lord of heaven and earth,
Help me pray as you yourself taught:
    "Our Father in heaven,
    hallowed be your name.
    Your kingdom come.

Your will be done,
on earth as it is in heaven.
Give us this day our daily bread.
And forgive us our debts,
as we also have forgiven our debtors.
And do not bring us to the time of trial,
but rescue us from the evil one."
(Matthew 6: 9-13)

From the foes of my land,
from the foes of my faith,
From the foes who would us dissever,
O Lord, preserve me, in life and in death,
With the Sign of the Cross for ever.
For the kingdom, the power, and the glory
are yours now and for ever. Amen.

Please proceed with "I beseech you, O Lord...," found after Option B.

Option B

O Jesus Christ,
Lord of heaven and earth,
Help me pray as you yourself taught:
Our Father in heaven,
hallowed be your name,
your kingdom come,
your will be done,
on earth as in heaven.
Give us today our daily bread.
Forgive us our sins
as we forgive those who sin against us.
Lead us not into temptation
but deliver us from evil.

From the foes of my land,
from the foes of my faith,
From the foes who would us dissever,
O Lord, preserve me, in life and in death,
With the Sign of the Cross for ever.
For the kingdom, the power, and the glory

are yours now and for ever. Amen.

I beseech you, O Lord.
God in Heaven, unsurpassed in power and might;
　　　Be behind me, Be on my left,
　　　Be before me, Be on my right!
Against each danger, you are my help;
In distress, upon you I call.
　　　In dark times, may you sustain me
　　　And lift me up again when I fall.
Lord over heaven and of earth,
You know my offenses.
　　　Yet, listening to my pleadings,
　　　You guide me away from sinful pretenses.
Lord of all creation and the many creatures,
You bestow on me many earthly treasures.
　　　Revealing love in each life and season,
　　　You share with me heavenly pleasures.
May you arouse me
In moments both of joy and of strife;
　　　Most holy Lord, bring me new life!

A Hymn, sung or heard (optional)

O Jesus Christ,
　　　Lord of heaven and earth,
　　　You are my riches, my store, my provision,
My star through the years
When troubles rend me,
　　　Through times of strife and tears,
　　　Sweet Jesus, defend me.

It was heavenly love impelled you
Thus to redeem our race,
　　　And bless my sight with the sweet light
　　　That shines from your face.

You to the stars ascended
Have banished fear, O Lord;
　　　Be yours all praise, through endless days.

Be you my sweet reward.

End this time of prayer by taking some time to bring to mind the various ways God shields you from harm or guides you through the world's tumult. Then, when you are ready, conclude by saying:

O Holy Lord, King in Heaven,
I place myself at the edge of your grace,
    On the floor of your house myself I place,
And to banish the sin of my heart away,
    I lower my knee to you this day.
Through life's torrents of pain may you bring me whole,
    And, O Lord Jesus Christ, preserve also my soul. Amen.

From Disciple to Friend

2.1   Let Thanks Arise On Every Side

a prayer on the Incarnation

Take a moment to quiet your spirit, becoming completely present to this time and place. Allow all other thoughts and concerns to fall away as you come into the presence of God. Then, when you are ready, begin.

Let thanks arise on every side
To Christ my help, my God of Might,
    Who has my body glorified
    And raised it to the throne of light.

Then let my heart with love o'erflow
My word and deeds be all of light,
    That when I leave these walks below,
    My soul shall climb the heavenly height.

A Hymn, sung or heard (optional)

Ancient of days, enthroned on high!
The Father unbegotten He,
    Whom space contains not, nor time,
    Who was and is and shall be:
And one-born Son, and Holy Ghost,
Who co-eternal glory share:
    One only God, of Persons Three,
    We praise, acknowledge, and declare.

Christ the Most High from heaven descends,
The Cross his sign and banner bright.
    The sun in darkness shrouds His face,
    The moon no more pours forth her light:
The stars upon the earth shall fall
As figs drop from the parent tree,
    When earth's broad space is bathed in fire,
    And men to dens and mountains flee.

Zeal of the Lord, consuming fire,
Shall 'whelm the foes, amazed and dumb,
Whose stony hearts will not receive
That Christ hath from the Father come:
But I shall soar my Lord to meet,
And so with him shall ever be,
To reap the due rewards amidst
The glories of Eternity.

A Psalm, read or recited

Holy Lord,
Under my thoughts may I God-thoughts find.
Half of my sins escape my mind.
For what I said, or did not say,
Pardon me, O Lord, I pray.

A Scriptural Selection, read aloud or quietly

O Lord, Jesus the Christ,
If I were in Heaven my harp I would sound
With apostles and angels and saints all around,
Praising and thanking the Son who is crowned,
May the poor race of Eve for that heaven be bound!

Holy Lord,
Descending from your throne above,
You sought the sluggish world to win,
Moved by the power of mighty love.
Lest earth be lost in death and sin.

Brought forth, a sacrifice divine
To expiate our deeds of doom,
Your way was through the sacred shrine
Of earth's most precious Virgin's womb.

O Holy Lord,
God with the Father and the Spirit,
For me is many a snare designed,
To fill my mind with doubts and fears;

Far from the land of holy saints,
I dwell within my vale of tears.
Let faith, let hope, let love —
Traits far above the cold world's way —
With patience, humility, and awe,
Become my guides from day to day.

I acknowledge, the evil I have done.
From the day of my birth till the day of my death,
Through the sight of my eyes,
Through the hearing of my ears,
Through the sayings of my mouth,
Through the thoughts of my heart,
Through the touch of my hands,
Through the course of my way,
Through all I said and did not,
Through all I promised and fulfilled not,
Through all the laws and holy commandments I broke.
I ask even now absolution of you,
For fear I may have never asked it as was right,
And that I might not live to ask it again,

O Holy Lord, my King in Heaven,
May you not let my soul stray from you,
May you keep me in a good state,
May you turn me toward what is good to do,
May you protect me from dangers, small and great.
May you fill my eyes with tears of repentance,
So I may avoid the sinner's awful sentence.
May the Grace of the God for ever be with me,
And whatever my needs, may the Triune God give me.

Select one of the following options for the Lord's Prayer.

Option A

O Jesus Christ,
Lord of heaven and earth,
Help me pray as you yourself taught:
"Our Father in heaven,

69

hallowed be your name.
Your kingdom come.
Your will be done,
on earth as it is in heaven.
Give us this day our daily bread.
And forgive us our debts,
as we also have forgiven our debtors.
And do not bring us to the time of trial,
but rescue us from the evil one."
(Matthew 6: 9-13)

From the foes of my land,
from the foes of my faith,
From the foes who would us dissever,

O Lord, preserve me, in life and in death,
With the Sign of the Cross for ever.
For the kingdom, the power, and the glory
are yours now and for ever. Amen.

Please proceed with "I beseech you, O Lord...," found after Option B.

Option B

O Jesus Christ,
Lord of heaven and earth,
Help me pray as you yourself taught:

Our Father in heaven,
hallowed be your name,
your kingdom come,
your will be done,
on earth as in heaven.
Give us today our daily bread.
Forgive us our sins
as we forgive those who sin against us.
Lead us not into temptation
but deliver us from evil.

From the foes of my land,
from the foes of my faith,
From the foes who would us dissever,

O Lord, preserve me, in life and in death,

With the Sign of the Cross for ever.
For the kingdom, the power, and the glory
are yours now and for ever. Amen.

I beseech you, O Lord.
God in Heaven, unsurpassed in power and might;
 Be behind me, Be on my left,
 Be before me, Be on my right!
Against each danger, you are my help;
In distress, upon you I call.
 In dark times, may you sustain me
 And lift me up again when I fall.
Lord over heaven and of earth,
You know my offenses.
 Yet, listening to my pleadings,
 You guide me away from sinful pretenses.
Lord of all creation and the many creatures,
You bestow on me many earthly treasures.
 Revealing love in each life and season,
 You share with me heavenly pleasures.
May you arouse me
In moments both of joy and of strife;
 Most holy Lord, bring me new life!

A Hymn, sung or heard (optional)

O Jesus Christ,
 Lord of heaven and earth,
 You are my riches, my store, my provision,
My star through the years
When troubles rend me,
 Through times of strife and tears,
 Sweet Jesus, defend me.

Your name is power; I call out "Save me!",
And lo, your glory shines aflame,
 While heaven and hell with trembling knee
 Bow down before your holy name.

To you I come, to you I cry,

O ruler of the judgment day;
Defend me by your grace, lest I
With powers of gloom be cast away.

End this time of prayer by taking some time to bring to mind the various ways God shields you from harm or guides you through the world's tumult. Then, when you are ready, conclude by saying:

O Holy Lord, King in Heaven,
I place myself at the edge of your grace,
On the floor of your house myself I place,
And to banish the sin of my heart away,
I lower my knee to you this day.
Through life's torrents of pain may you bring me whole,
And, O Lord Jesus Christ, preserve also my soul. Amen.

2.2   Behold The Lamb! He Comes.

a prayer on Jesus' nativity

Take a moment to quiet your spirit, becoming completely present to this time and place. Allow all other thoughts and concerns to fall away as you come into the presence of God. Then, when you are ready, begin.

Behold the Lamb! he comes to bear
From all the world its load of sin;
  O let me in haste, in humble prayer,
  Strive his loving grace to win.

Shine out, O wondrous star, on high,
Enclose the world in flaming light,
  Let me not fall in guilt and die;
  Lord, guard and guide my steps aright.

A Hymn, sung or heard (optional)

On lowly bed of hay he lies,
His palace but a stable poor;
  The God that rules the earth and skies
  Does all our wants and woes endure.

The angel choirs rejoice on high,
Through radiant skies their voices ring,
  The shepherds see the blazing sky,
  And bow before the Infant King.

The Magi follow through the night
The mystic star that goes before;
  By light, they seek the Lord of Light,
  The King and God whom they adore.

All praise and power and glory be
To Jesus whom the Virgin bore;
  To you, Father, equal is he

And to the Spirit, evermore.

A Psalm, read or recited

Holy Lord,
Under my thoughts may I God-thoughts find.
Half of my sins escape my mind.
  For what I said, or did not say,
  Pardon me, O Lord, I pray.

A Scriptural Selection, read aloud or quietly

O Lord, Jesus the Christ,
If I were in Heaven my harp I would sound
With apostles and angels and saints all around,
  Praising and thanking the Son who is crowned,
  May the poor race of Eve for that heaven be bound!

Remember, O Creator Lord,
That from the stainless Virgin's womb
  The flesh of man you did assume
  To save man's flesh from guilt abhorred.

And lo, this day that gave you birth
Shall glorify your holy name,
  Who from the Father's bosom came,
  Sole Son and Saviour of the earth.

The heavens, the earth, the rolling seas,
And all that live beneath the skies
  Uplift to you adoring eyes
  And hail you with new harmonies.

O Holy Lord,
  God with the Father and the Spirit,
For me is many a snare designed,
To fill my mind with doubts and fears;
  Far from the land of holy saints,
  I dwell within my vale of tears.
Let faith, let hope, let love —

Traits far above the cold world's way —
　　　　With patience, humility, and awe,
　　　　Become my guides from day to day.

I acknowledge, the evil I have done.
From the day of my birth till the day of my death,
　　　　Through the sight of my eyes,
Through the hearing of my ears,
　　　　Through the sayings of my mouth,
Through the thoughts of my heart,
　　　　Through the touch of my hands,
Through the course of my way,
　　　　Through all I said and did not,
Through all I promised and fulfilled not,
　　　　Through all the laws and holy commandments I broke.
I ask even now absolution of you,
　　　　For fear I may have never asked it as was right,
　　　　And that I might not live to ask it again,

O Holy Lord, my King in Heaven,
May you not let my soul stray from you,
May you keep me in a good state,
　　　　May you turn me toward what is good to do,
　　　　May you protect me from dangers, small and great.
May you fill my eyes with tears of repentance,
　　　　So I may avoid the sinner's awful sentence.
May the Grace of the God for ever be with me,
　　　　And whatever my needs, may the Triune God give me.

Select one of the following options for the Lord's Prayer.

Option A

O Jesus Christ,
Lord of heaven and earth,
Help me pray as you yourself taught:
　　　　"Our Father in heaven,
　　　　hallowed be your name.
　　　　Your kingdom come.
　　　　Your will be done,

on earth as it is in heaven.
Give us this day our daily bread.
And forgive us our debts,
as we also have forgiven our debtors.
And do not bring us to the time of trial,
but rescue us from the evil one."
(Matthew 6: 9-13)
From the foes of my land,
from the foes of my faith,
From the foes who would us dissever,
O Lord, preserve me, in life and in death,
With the Sign of the Cross for ever.
For the kingdom, the power, and the glory
are yours now and for ever. Amen.

Please proceed with "I beseech you, O Lord...," found after Option B.

Option B

O Jesus Christ,
Lord of heaven and earth,
Help me pray as you yourself taught:
Our Father in heaven,
hallowed be your name,
your kingdom come,
your will be done,
on earth as in heaven.
Give us today our daily bread.
Forgive us our sins
as we forgive those who sin against us.
Lead us not into temptation
but deliver us from evil.
From the foes of my land,
from the foes of my faith,
From the foes who would us dissever,
O Lord, preserve me, in life and in death,
With the Sign of the Cross for ever.
For the kingdom, the power, and the glory
are yours now and for ever. Amen.

I beseech you, O Lord.
God in Heaven, unsurpassed in power and might;
Be behind me, Be on my left,
Be before me, Be on my right!
Against each danger, you are my help;
In distress, upon you I call.
In dark times, may you sustain me
And lift me up again when I fall.
Lord over heaven and of earth,
You know my offenses.
Yet, listening to my pleadings,
You guide me away from sinful pretenses.
Lord of all creation and the many creatures,
You bestow on me many earthly treasures.
Revealing love in each life and season,
You share with me heavenly pleasures.
May you arouse me
In moments both of joy and of strife;
Most holy Lord, bring me new life!

A Hymn, sung or heard (optional)

O Jesus Christ,
Lord of heaven and earth,
You are my riches, my store, my provision,
My star through the years
When troubles rend me,
Through times of strife and tears,
Sweet Jesus, defend me.

Jesus, Reedemer of the earth,
Begotten by the God of light,
Equal in majesty and might,
Before the day-star had its birth;

The splendour of the Father on high,
Of humankind the living hope,
Aid all that under heaven's cope
To embrace the joys you supply!

End this time of prayer by taking some time to bring to mind the various ways God shields you from harm or guides you through the world's tumult. Then, when you are ready, conclude by saying:

O Holy Lord, King in Heaven,
I place myself at the edge of your grace,
    On the floor of your house myself I place,
And to banish the sin of my heart away,
    I lower my knee to you this day.
Through life's torrents of pain may you bring me whole,
   And, O Lord Jesus Christ, preserve also my soul. Amen.

2.3   Gentle Jesus, Fount Of Healing

a prayer for spiritual guidance and renewal

Take a moment to quiet your spirit, becoming completely present to this time and place. Allow all other thoughts and concerns to fall away as you come into the presence of God. Then, when you are ready, begin.

Gentle Jesus, fount of healing,
Solace unto souls appealing
By the mildness of your grace,
> Calm my restless mind, and render
> Soothing thoughts therein and tender;
> Pride and bitterness efface.

By your fostering care provided
All my life shall thus be guided,
Safe in faith, from evil free;
> Kindled by your kindness, never
> From your love my soul shall sever,
> All my desires in you shall be.

A Hymn, sung or heard (optional)

My God, my life, my love, my light,
My strength, my joy, my treasure,
> Let it be my thought both day and night
> In you to take my pleasure.
Increase my love, as I sigh and groan
> My careless lips to move it,
> And let my thoughts be fixed alone
On right living, with all sins abhorred.

Blot out my crimes and me forgive,
O Lord do not deny me,
> And grant my thoughts for ever be
> On Jesus Crucified.
In honour of your passion's sake,

This new year's gift bestow me,
That I into protection take
Sweet Jesus, my King and Lord.

To God the Father glory be,
For his mercy still I crave,
    And to His Son who died for me
    Who spilt his blood to me save.
And to the Holy Ghost all three.
They on us bestow gifts and grace,
    And should our thoughts for ever be
    That the Godhead's love we embrace.

A Psalm, read or recited

Holy Lord,
Under my thoughts may I God-thoughts find.
Half of my sins escape my mind.
    For what I said, or did not say,
    Pardon me, O Lord, I pray.

A Scriptural Selection, read aloud or quietly

O Lord, Jesus the Christ,
If I were in Heaven my harp I would sound
With apostles and angels and saints all around,
    Praising and thanking the Son who is crowned,
    May the poor race of Eve for that heaven be bound!

Holy Lord,
Now since I am come to the brink of death
And my latest breath must soon be drawn,
    May heaven, though late, be my aim and mark
    From day till dark, and from dark till dawn.

O Jesus Christ, who has died for men,
And has risen again without stain or spot,
    Unto those who have sought it, you show the way,
    Oh why, in my days, have I sought it not!

O Holy Lord,
    God with the Father and the Spirit,
For me is many a snare designed,
To fill my mind with doubts and fears;
        Far from the land of holy saints,
        I dwell within my vale of tears.
Let faith, let hope, let love —
Traits far above the cold world's way —
        With patience, humility, and awe,
        Become my guides from day to day.

I acknowledge, the evil I have done.
From the day of my birth till the day of my death,
    Through the sight of my eyes,
Through the hearing of my ears,
    Through the sayings of my mouth,
Through the thoughts of my heart,
    Through the touch of my hands,
Through the course of my way,
    Through all I said and did not,
Through all I promised and fulfilled not,
    Through all the laws and holy commandments I broke.
I ask even now absolution of you,
    For fear I may have never asked it as was right,
    And that I might not live to ask it again,

O Holy Lord, my King in Heaven,
May you not let my soul stray from you,
May you keep me in a good state,
    May you turn me toward what is good to do,
    May you protect me from dangers, small and great.
May you fill my eyes with tears of repentance,
    So I may avoid the sinner's awful sentence.
May the Grace of the God for ever be with me,
    And whatever my needs, may the Triune God give me.

Select one of the following options for the Lord's Prayer.

Option A

O Jesus Christ,
Lord of heaven and earth,
Help me pray as you yourself taught:
>"*Our Father in heaven,*
>*hallowed be your name.*
>*Your kingdom come.*
>*Your will be done,*
>*on earth as it is in heaven.*
>*Give us this day our daily bread.*
>*And forgive us our debts,*
>*as we also have forgiven our debtors.*
>*And do not bring us to the time of trial,*
>*but rescue us from the evil one."*
>*(Matthew 6: 9-13)*

From the foes of my land,
from the foes of my faith,
From the foes who would us dissever,
>O Lord, preserve me, in life and in death,
>With the Sign of the Cross for ever.
>*For the kingdom, the power, and the glory*
>*are yours now and for ever. Amen.*

Please proceed with "I beseech you, O Lord...," found after Option B.

Option B

O Jesus Christ,
Lord of heaven and earth,
Help me pray as you yourself taught:
>*Our Father in heaven,*
>*hallowed be your name,*
>*your kingdom come,*
>*your will be done,*
>*on earth as in heaven.*
>*Give us today our daily bread.*
>*Forgive us our sins*
>*as we forgive those who sin against us.*
>*Lead us not into temptation*
>*but deliver us from evil.*

From the foes of my land,
from the foes of my faith,
From the foes who would us dissever,
  O Lord, preserve me, in life and in death,
  With the Sign of the Cross for ever.
  For the kingdom, the power, and the glory
  are yours now and for ever. Amen.

I beseech you, O Lord.
God in Heaven, unsurpassed in power and might;
  Be behind me, Be on my left,
  Be before me, Be on my right!
Against each danger, you are my help;
In distress, upon you I call.
  In dark times, may you sustain me
  And lift me up again when I fall.
Lord over heaven and of earth,
You know my offenses.
  Yet, listening to my pleadings,
  You guide me away from sinful pretenses.
Lord of all creation and the many creatures,
You bestow on me many earthly treasures.
  Revealing love in each life and season,
  You share with me heavenly pleasures.
May you arouse me
In moments both of joy and of strife;
  Most holy Lord, bring me new life!

A Hymn, sung or heard (optional)

O Jesus Christ,
  Lord of heaven and earth,
  You are my riches, my store, my provision,
My star through the years
When troubles rend me,
  Through times of strife and tears,
  Sweet Jesus, defend me.

Gentle Jesus, Fount of pleasure,
Be your love my dearest treasure,

Let my soul your passion feel;
  Be that passion faith's foundation,
  Love's desire and recreation,
  And of hope the sign and seal.

Cleanse my heart from evil yearning,
Fire therein a holy burning,
For the blessed life above;
  In the end to me be given,
  Lord, eternal joy in heaven
  As a comrade in your love.

End this time of prayer by taking some time to bring to mind the various ways God shields you from harm or guides you through the world's tumult. Then, when you are ready, conclude by saying:

O Holy Lord, King in Heaven,
I place myself at the edge of your grace,
  On the floor of your house myself I place,
And to banish the sin of my heart away,
  I lower my knee to you this day.
Through life's torrents of pain may you bring me whole,
  And, O Lord Jesus Christ, preserve also my soul. Amen.

2.4 Dear Redeemer, Loved And Loving

a prayer of praise for Jesus' redemptive mission

Take a moment to quiet your spirit, becoming completely present to this time and place. Allow all other thoughts and concerns to fall away as you come into the presence of God. Then, when you are ready, begin.

Dear Redeemer, loved and loving,
All my faith I place in you;
your undying truths you teach,
      With unfailing force to me,
      Come in tender love, my Saviour;
      Fill with faith the fragile breast;
Lift my spirit to your comfort,
      Let me find in you sweet rest.

O my loving Lord, I love you
More than all things here below;
      I renounce whate'er offends you,
      Fling it from me as a foe.
Heaven and earth bow down before you,
And in all, your love I see;
      Let me cleave to you forever
      And, dear Lord, cleave you to me.

A Hymn, sung or heard (optional)

Jesus, our heavenly Lord and King,
You did the world's salvation bring,
      And by your death upon the tree,
      Did out of bondage make us free.

Hear now our prayers, O Son of God,
Preserve the gifts your hand bestowed,
      Unto your love all nations draw,
      And bring mankind to know your law.

The tongues of all creation call
And hail your name as Lord of all:
    Their life arose from God's command,
    Their living hope, from your right hand.

The Father's luminous thrones above,
With beating wings and words of love,
    The cherubim and seraphim,
    Sing out to you their ceaseless hymn.

They sing to you in sweet accord,
Their, "Holy, holy, holy Lord";
    Great God of hosts and victories,
    your glory fills the earth and skies.

A Psalm, read or recited

Holy Lord,
Under my thoughts may I God-thoughts find.
Half of my sins escape my mind.
    For what I said, or did not say,
    Pardon me, O Lord, I pray.

A Scriptural Selection, read aloud or quietly

O Lord, Jesus the Christ,
If I were in Heaven my harp I would sound
With apostles and angels and saints all around,
    Praising and thanking the Son who is crowned,
    May the poor race of Eve for that heaven be bound!

Holy Lord,
Amid heavenly splendors ranged on high,
To you angelic choirs outcry;
    And bands of bright archangels praise
    Your name in never-ending lays.

Lord, guide me by your blessed light,
And bring me to your heavenly height,
    Enroll me with your blessed throng

To sing your praise in deathless song.

O Holy Lord,
     God with the Father and the Spirit,
For me is many a snare designed,
To fill my mind with doubts and fears;
     Far from the land of holy saints,
     I dwell within my vale of tears.
Let faith, let hope, let love —
Traits far above the cold world's way —
     With patience, humility, and awe,
     Become my guides from day to day.

I acknowledge, the evil I have done.
From the day of my birth till the day of my death,
     Through the sight of my eyes,
Through the hearing of my ears,
     Through the sayings of my mouth,
Through the thoughts of my heart,
     Through the touch of my hands,
Through the course of my way,
     Through all I said and did not,
Through all I promised and fulfilled not,
     Through all the laws and holy commandments I broke.
I ask even now absolution of you,
     For fear I may have never asked it as was right,
     And that I might not live to ask it again,

O Holy Lord, my King in Heaven,
May you not let my soul stray from you,
May you keep me in a good state,
     May you turn me toward what is good to do,
     May you protect me from dangers, small and great.
May you fill my eyes with tears of repentance,
     So I may avoid the sinner's awful sentence.
May the Grace of the God for ever be with me,
     And whatever my needs, may the Triune God give me.

Select one of the following options for the Lord's Prayer.

Option A

O Jesus Christ,
Lord of heaven and earth,
Help me pray as you yourself taught:
> "Our Father in heaven,
> hallowed be your name.
> Your kingdom come.
> Your will be done,
> on earth as it is in heaven.
> Give us this day our daily bread.
> And forgive us our debts,
> as we also have forgiven our debtors.
> And do not bring us to the time of trial,
> but rescue us from the evil one."
> (Matthew 6: 9-13)

From the foes of my land,
from the foes of my faith,
From the foes who would us dissever,
> O Lord, preserve me, in life and in death,
> With the Sign of the Cross for ever.
> For the kingdom, the power, and the glory
> are yours now and for ever. Amen.

Please proceed with "I beseech you, O Lord...," found after Option B.

Option B

O Jesus Christ,
Lord of heaven and earth,
Help me pray as you yourself taught:
> Our Father in heaven,
> hallowed be your name,
> your kingdom come,
> your will be done,
> on earth as in heaven.
> Give us today our daily bread.
> Forgive us our sins
> as we forgive those who sin against us.

Lead us not into temptation
but deliver us from evil.
From the foes of my land,
from the foes of my faith,
From the foes who would us dissever,
O Lord, preserve me, in life and in death,
With the Sign of the Cross for ever.
For the kingdom, the power, and the glory
are yours now and for ever. Amen.

I beseech you, O Lord.
God in Heaven, unsurpassed in power and might;
Be behind me, Be on my left,
Be before me, Be on my right!
Against each danger, you are my help;
In distress, upon you I call.
In dark times, may you sustain me
And lift me up again when I fall.
Lord over heaven and of earth,
You know my offenses.
Yet, listening to my pleadings,
You guide me away from sinful pretenses.
Lord of all creation and the many creatures,
You bestow on me many earthly treasures.
Revealing love in each life and season,
You share with me heavenly pleasures.
May you arouse me
In moments both of joy and of strife;
Most holy Lord, bring me new life!

A Hymn, sung or heard (optional)

O Jesus Christ,
Lord of heaven and earth,
You are my riches, my store, my provision,
My star through the years
When troubles rend me,
Through times of strife and tears,
Sweet Jesus, defend me.

Behold, the shadows fly the dawn,
Night yields unto the star of day;
> So may the shades of vice be gone,
> And every stain be washed away.

Hear me, dear Lord, while day is young,
Banish, I pray, all guilt and crime,
> And let your love by every tongue
> Be sung unto the end of time.

> *End this time of prayer by taking some time to bring to mind*
the various ways God shields you from harm or guides you through
the world's tumult. Then, when you are ready, conclude by saying:

O Holy Lord, King in Heaven,
I place myself at the edge of your grace,
> On the floor of your house myself I place,
And to banish the sin of my heart away,
> I lower my knee to you this day.
Through life's torrents of pain may you bring me whole,
> And, O Lord Jesus Christ, preserve also my soul. Amen.

a humble petition to enter God's Kingdom

Take a moment to quiet your spirit, becoming completely present to this time and place. Allow all other thoughts and concerns to fall away as you come into the presence of God. Then, when you are ready, begin.

Hear me, Christ, my King,
      Hear you the praise I bring,
      And lead me on;
In tender mercy bend,
My soul from harm defend,
      And let my hopes ascend
      Unto your throne.

Upon the road of life
Keep me from stain and strife
In your sweet care;
      Extend your right hand, Lord,
      Your gracious aid afford,
Be you my watch and ward;
      Lord, hear my prayer.

A Hymn, sung or heard (optional)

'Til the Trinity thought, and thinking pitied
The race that was lying beneath the rod,
      And the Son of Grace came down through space
      To the womb of Mary Mother of God.

If your neighbour offend you, O passion's slave,
You will not forgive him, through spite and pride,
      Yet see how the Son of Grace forgave
      The person who pierced God's holy side.

The heart that abhors its earthly neighbour
As a brimstone lump in the breast shall lie,

And the perjured tongue, that is loosely hung,
Like a salted flame in the mouth shall fry.

At the hour of doom, on the awful Mount
We all must gather beneath God's eye,
    And the priest for his flock give a sharp account,
    And account for the tares in his wheat and rye.

Is it not little we think about the grace of the Son,
And how he was tortured in our place
    And so forgiveness of the sin of Adam won —
    Ending humankind's sorrowful disgrace.

A Psalm, read or recited

Holy Lord,
Under my thoughts may I God-thoughts find.
Half of my sins escape my mind.
    For what I said, or did not say,
    Pardon me, O Lord, I pray.

A Scriptural Selection, read aloud or quietly

O Lord, Jesus the Christ,
If I were in Heaven my harp I would sound
With apostles and angels and saints all around,
    Praising and thanking the Son who is crowned,
    May the poor race of Eve for that heaven be bound!

Holy Lord,
Glory and honour and lasting praise,
Through endless days to the Son of God,
    You have bought your glory, dear Lord,
    With sweat of brow and fume of blood.

Through toilsome years thrice ten and three,
Each day to you was the poor man's day,
    Teaching and learning all his needs,
    On the road that leads the heavenly way.

O Holy Lord,
> God with the Father and the Spirit,
For me is many a snare designed,
To fill my mind with doubts and fears;
>> Far from the land of holy saints,
>> I dwell within my vale of tears.
Let faith, let hope, let love —
Traits far above the cold world's way —
>> With patience, humility, and awe,
>> Become my guides from day to day.

I acknowledge, the evil I have done.
From the day of my birth till the day of my death,
> Through the sight of my eyes,
Through the hearing of my ears,
> Through the sayings of my mouth,
Through the thoughts of my heart,
> Through the touch of my hands,
Through the course of my way,
> Through all I said and did not,
Through all I promised and fulfilled not,
> Through all the laws and holy commandments I broke.
I ask even now absolution of you,
> For fear I may have never asked it as was right,
> And that I might not live to ask it again,

O Holy Lord, my King in Heaven,
May you not let my soul stray from you,
May you keep me in a good state,
> May you turn me toward what is good to do,
> May you protect me from dangers, small and great.
May you fill my eyes with tears of repentance,
> So I may avoid the sinner's awful sentence.
May the Grace of the God for ever be with me,
> And whatever my needs, may the Triune God give me.

Select one of the following options for the Lord's Prayer.

Option A

O Jesus Christ,
Lord of heaven and earth,
Help me pray as you yourself taught:
> *"Our Father in heaven,*
> *hallowed be your name.*
> *Your kingdom come.*
> *Your will be done,*
> *on earth as it is in heaven.*
> *Give us this day our daily bread.*
> *And forgive us our debts,*
> *as we also have forgiven our debtors.*
> *And do not bring us to the time of trial,*
> *but rescue us from the evil one."*
> *(Matthew 6: 9-13)*

From the foes of my land,
from the foes of my faith,
From the foes who would us dissever,
> O Lord, preserve me, in life and in death,
> With the Sign of the Cross for ever.
> *For the kingdom, the power, and the glory*
> *are yours now and for ever. Amen.*

Please proceed with "I beseech you, O Lord...," found after Option B.

Option B

O Jesus Christ,
Lord of heaven and earth,
Help me pray as you yourself taught:
> *Our Father in heaven,*
> *hallowed be your name,*
> *your kingdom come,*
> *your will be done,*
> *on earth as in heaven.*
> *Give us today our daily bread.*
> *Forgive us our sins*
> *as we forgive those who sin against us.*
> *Lead us not into temptation*
> *but deliver us from evil.*

94

From the foes of my land,
from the foes of my faith,
From the foes who would us dissever,
> O Lord, preserve me, in life and in death,
> With the Sign of the Cross for ever.
> *For the kingdom, the power, and the glory*
> *are yours now and for ever. Amen.*

I beseech you, O Lord.
God in Heaven, unsurpassed in power and might;
> Be behind me, Be on my left,
> Be before me, Be on my right!
Against each danger, you are my help;
In distress, upon you I call.
> In dark times, may you sustain me
> And lift me up again when I fall.
Lord over heaven and of earth,
You know my offenses.
> Yet, listening to my pleadings,
> You guide me away from sinful pretenses.
Lord of all creation and the many creatures,
You bestow on me many earthly treasures.
> Revealing love in each life and season,
> You share with me heavenly pleasures.
May you arouse me
In moments both of joy and of strife;
> Most holy Lord, bring me new life!

A Hymn, sung or heard (optional)

O Jesus Christ,
> Lord of heaven and earth,
> You are my riches, my store, my provision,
My star through the years
When troubles rend me,
> Through times of strife and tears,
> Sweet Jesus, defend me.

All lingering shadows from my mind expel,
With dreams and motions that in darkness dwell,

My bosom purge of all that brings stain,
And bathe my spirit in your crystal well.

Within my soul let saving faith find place,
Let hope draw radiance from your tender face.
And let my heart in brotherhood expand
The love of God and neighbour; grant this grace.

End this time of prayer by taking some time to bring to mind the various ways God shields you from harm or guides you through the world's tumult. Then, when you are ready, conclude by saying:

O Holy Lord, King in Heaven,
I place myself at the edge of your grace,
On the floor of your house myself I place,
And to banish the sin of my heart away,
I lower my knee to you this day.
Through life's torrents of pain may you bring me whole,
And, O Lord Jesus Christ, preserve also my soul. Amen.

a prayer on the demands of following Jesus

Take a moment to quiet your spirit, becoming completely present to this time and place. Allow all other thoughts and concerns to fall away as you come into the presence of God. Then, when you are ready, begin.

The Victor, Christ, with flag unfurled
Brings triumph o'er the sinful world,
> The king of darkness quells, and opes
> The gates of heaven to human hopes.

Dear Jesus, bring us purity,
That you our paschal joy may be;
> Be with us always; let your love
> Illume our spirits from above.

A Hymn, sung or heard (optional)

Remember, O friend, your end of sorrow,
Spend not your time with lies and folly,
> Forsake the world troubled and hollow,
> Sweet at the first but worse shall follow.

Though strong you are and smart and smiling,
Full of wealth and health, most lively,
> Make no boast, the whole are lying
> Unsubstantial shadows flying.

Though plenty of gold you hold and jewels,
Şilver white, brass bright, and pewter,
> Sheep and kind, with swine ground-rooting,
> Castles and holds of untold-of beauty.

Take no heed of the creed or the wealth of the world,
Do not boast of its host or its banners unfurled,
> you art made out of clay, into clay to be turned,

And into the room of the tomb to be hurled.

Holy Lord,
Under my thoughts may I God-thoughts find.
Half of my sins escape my mind.
>For what I said, or did not say,
>Pardon me, O Lord, I pray.

A Scriptural Selection, read aloud or quietly

O Lord, Jesus the Christ,
If I were in Heaven my harp I would sound
With apostles and angels and saints all around,
>Praising and thanking the Son who is crowned,
>May the poor race of Eve for that heaven be bound!

Holy Lord,
To the Trinity's presence the soul must mount,
To the judgments it comes, and its sins it bears,
>And nought that it pleads for itself shall count
>Save fastings, and givings of alms, and prayers.

If you gave but a glass of the water cold,
(The simplest drink on the green earth's sod)
>Your reward is before you, a thousand-fold,
>If the thing has been done for the sake of God.

Three things there be, the reward of man
For offending God — 'tis a risk to run —
>Misfortune's fall, and a shortened span,
>And the pains of hell when all is done.

O Holy Lord,
>God with the Father and the Spirit,
For me is many a snare designed,
To fill my mind with doubts and fears;
>Far from the land of holy saints,
>I dwell within my vale of tears.

Let faith, let hope, let love —
Traits far above the cold world's way —
      With patience, humility, and awe,
      Become my guides from day to day.

I acknowledge, the evil I have done.
From the day of my birth till the day of my death,
      Through the sight of my eyes,
Through the hearing of my ears,
      Through the sayings of my mouth,
Through the thoughts of my heart,
      Through the touch of my hands,
Through the course of my way,
      Through all I said and did not,
Through all I promised and fulfilled not,
      Through all the laws and holy commandments I broke.
I ask even now absolution of you,
      For fear I may have never asked it as was right,
      And that I might not live to ask it again,

O Holy Lord, my King in Heaven,
May you not let my soul stray from you,
May you keep me in a good state,
      May you turn me toward what is good to do,
      May you protect me from dangers, small and great.
May you fill my eyes with tears of repentance,
      So I may avoid the sinner's awful sentence.
May the Grace of the God for ever be with me,
      And whatever my needs, may the Triune God give me.

Select one of the following options for the Lord's Prayer.

Option A

O Jesus Christ,
Lord of heaven and earth,
Help me pray as you yourself taught:
      "Our Father in heaven,
      hallowed be your name.
      Your kingdom come.

Your will be done,
on earth as it is in heaven.
Give us this day our daily bread.
And forgive us our debts,
as we also have forgiven our debtors.
And do not bring us to the time of trial,
but rescue us from the evil one."
(Matthew 6: 9-13)
From the foes of my land,
from the foes of my faith,
From the foes who would us dissever,
> O Lord, preserve me, in life and in death,
> With the Sign of the Cross for ever.
> *For the kingdom, the power, and the glory*
> *are yours now and for ever. Amen.*

Please proceed with "I beseech you, O Lord...," found after Option B.

Option B

O Jesus Christ,
Lord of heaven and earth,
Help me pray as you yourself taught:
> *Our Father in heaven,*
> *hallowed be your name,*
> *your kingdom come,*
> *your will be done,*
> *on earth as in heaven.*
> *Give us today our daily bread.*
> *Forgive us our sins*
> *as we forgive those who sin against us.*
> *Lead us not into temptation*
> *but deliver us from evil.*
From the foes of my land,
from the foes of my faith,
From the foes who would us dissever,
> O Lord, preserve me, in life and in death,
> With the Sign of the Cross for ever.
> *For the kingdom, the power, and the glory*

are yours now and for ever. Amen.

I beseech you, O Lord.
God in Heaven, unsurpassed in power and might;
      Be behind me, Be on my left,
      Be before me, Be on my right!
Against each danger, you are my help;
In distress, upon you I call.
      In dark times, may you sustain me
      And lift me up again when I fall.
Lord over heaven and of earth,
You know my offenses.
      Yet, listening to my pleadings,
      You guide me away from sinful pretenses.
Lord of all creation and the many creatures,
You bestow on me many earthly treasures.
      Revealing love in each life and season,
      You share with me heavenly pleasures.
May you arouse me
In moments both of joy and of strife;
      Most holy Lord, bring me new life!

A Hymn, sung or heard (optional)

O Jesus Christ,
      Lord of heaven and earth,
      You are my riches, my store, my provision,
My star through the years
When troubles rend me,
      Through times of strife and tears,
      Sweet Jesus, defend me.

Be you my lasting joy, O Lord,
My love on earth, my high reward;
      Kind Ruler of the world, inspire
      My longing soul with holy fire.
To you I bow my heart in prayer,
Lord, keep me from the tempter's snare;
      Lift up my soul with heavenly grace,
      And fit me for your dwelling-place.

End this time of prayer by taking some time to bring to mind the various ways God shields you from harm or guides you through the world's tumult. Then, when you are ready, conclude by saying:

O Holy Lord, King in Heaven,
I place myself at the edge of your grace,
     On the floor of your house myself I place,
And to banish the sin of my heart away,
     I lower my knee to you this day.
Through life's torrents of pain may you bring me whole,
    And, O Lord Jesus Christ, preserve also my soul. Amen.

a prayer in praise of Jesus' power and majesty

Take a moment to quiet your spirit, becoming completely present to this time and place. Allow all other thoughts and concerns to fall away as you come into the presence of God. Then, when you are ready, begin.

You are, O Christ, my health and light,
The power that glorifies the sun,
> That veils with deepening shades the night,
> And gives each star its course to run.

No wandering thought or vain desire
Be near my soul to soil or stain,
> But kindled by the holy fire
> Of love for you, with you remain.

A Hymn, sung or heard (optional)

O you who seek the Christ to find,
Uplift your eyes on high;
> For lo! to every humble mind
> His glory fills the sky.

His mighty wonders there behold,
In boundless fields of light,
> Sublime, eternal, and as old
> As heaven and ancient night.

Here is the nation's King indeed,
Here Israel's mighty Lord,
> To Abraham promised and his seed,
> Forevermore adored.

To him each prophet did witness,
By word and sign sincere;
> Blessed by the Father, saying in sweetness,

"Behold, believe and hear!"

To Jesus, who his light displays
To babes, all glory be,
    To Father and Spirit equal praise
    For all eternity.

A Psalm, read or recited

Holy Lord,
Under my thoughts may I God-thoughts find.
Half of my sins escape my mind.
    For what I said, or did not say,
    Pardon me, O Lord, I pray.

A Scriptural Selection, read aloud or quietly

O Lord, Jesus the Christ,
If I were in Heaven my harp I would sound
With apostles and angels and saints all around,
    Praising and thanking the Son who is crowned,
    May the poor race of Eve for that heaven be bound!

Holy Lord,
Be my heart and hopes renewed
In light and love and gratitude,
    So, illumed by you, may my actions
    Worthily fulfill your loving intentions.

I praise you, Lord, forevermore;
With the Father, who I also adore,
    And with the Spirit, three in one,
    Reigning while endless ages run.

O Holy Lord,
    God with the Father and the Spirit,
For me is many a snare designed,
To fill my mind with doubts and fears;
    Far from the land of holy saints,
    I dwell within my vale of tears.

Let faith, let hope, let love —
Traits far above the cold world's way —
    With patience, humility, and awe,
    Become my guides from day to day.

I acknowledge, the evil I have done.
From the day of my birth till the day of my death,
    Through the sight of my eyes,
Through the hearing of my ears,
    Through the sayings of my mouth,
Through the thoughts of my heart,
    Through the touch of my hands,
Through the course of my way,
    Through all I said and did not,
Through all I promised and fulfilled not,
    Through all the laws and holy commandments I broke.
I ask even now absolution of you,
    For fear I may have never asked it as was right,
    And that I might not live to ask it again,

O Holy Lord, my King in Heaven,
May you not let my soul stray from you,
May you keep me in a good state,
    May you turn me toward what is good to do,
    May you protect me from dangers, small and great.
May you fill my eyes with tears of repentance,
    So I may avoid the sinner's awful sentence.
May the Grace of the God for ever be with me,
    And whatever my needs, may the Triune God give me.

Select one of the following options for the Lord's Prayer.

Option A

O Jesus Christ,
Lord of heaven and earth,
Help me pray as you yourself taught:
    "Our Father in heaven,
    hallowed be your name.
    Your kingdom come.

Your will be done,
on earth as it is in heaven.
Give us this day our daily bread.
And forgive us our debts,
as we also have forgiven our debtors.
And do not bring us to the time of trial,
but rescue us from the evil one."
(Matthew 6: 9-13)

From the foes of my land,
from the foes of my faith,
From the foes who would us dissever,
O Lord, preserve me, in life and in death,
With the Sign of the Cross for ever.
For the kingdom, the power, and the glory
are yours now and for ever. Amen.

Please proceed with "I beseech you, O Lord...," found after Option B.

Option B

O Jesus Christ,
Lord of heaven and earth,
Help me pray as you yourself taught:
Our Father in heaven,
hallowed be your name,
your kingdom come,
your will be done,
on earth as in heaven.
Give us today our daily bread.
Forgive us our sins
as we forgive those who sin against us.
Lead us not into temptation
but deliver us from evil.

From the foes of my land,
from the foes of my faith,
From the foes who would us dissever,
O Lord, preserve me, in life and in death,
With the Sign of the Cross for ever.
For the kingdom, the power, and the glory

are yours now and for ever. Amen.

I beseech you, O Lord.
God in Heaven, unsurpassed in power and might;
    Be behind me, Be on my left,
    Be before me, Be on my right!
Against each danger, you are my help;
In distress, upon you I call.
    In dark times, may you sustain me
    And lift me up again when I fall.
Lord over heaven and of earth,
You know my offenses.
    Yet, listening to my pleadings,
    You guide me away from sinful pretenses.
Lord of all creation and the many creatures,
You bestow on me many earthly treasures.
    Revealing love in each life and season,
    You share with me heavenly pleasures.
May you arouse me
In moments both of joy and of strife;
    Most holy Lord, bring me new life!

A Hymn, sung or heard (optional)

O Jesus Christ,
    Lord of heaven and earth,
    You are my riches, my store, my provision,
My star through the years
When troubles rend me,
    Through times of strife and tears,
    Sweet Jesus, defend me.

O you who seek the Lord, come nigh,
To heaven uplift your reverent eyes,
    The Royal Banner of our God
    Is blazoned on the midnight skies.

O Jesus, to the world revealed!
To you let glory ever be,
    To Father and to Holy Ghost,

From age to age eternally.

End this time of prayer by taking some time to bring to mind the various ways God shields you from harm or guides you through the world's tumult. Then, when you are ready, conclude by saying:

O Holy Lord, King in Heaven,
I place myself at the edge of your grace,
    On the floor of your house myself I place,
And to banish the sin of my heart away,
    I lower my knee to you this day.
Through life's torrents of pain may you bring me whole,
    And, O Lord Jesus Christ, preserve also my soul. Amen.

2.8   Oh, Kind Creator Of the Skies

a prayer of Christian fellowship

Take a moment to quiet your spirit, becoming completely present to this time and place. Allow all other thoughts and concerns to fall away as you come into the presence of God. Then, when you are ready, begin.

Oh, kind Creator of the skies,
Eternal light to guide my feet,
       Give ear to my beseeching cries
       And save me in your mercy sweet.

Descending from your throne above,
You strive the sluggish world to win,
       Moved by the power of mighty love,
       Lest earth be lost in death and sin.

A Hymn, sung or heard (optional)

To my Friends, remember what I say,
that in the day of Judgement's shock,
       when all ghosts ambling down the Mount,
       the sheep may count you of their flock.

And narrow though you find the path
To heaven's high wrath, and hard to gain,
       I warn you shun that broad white road
       That leads to the abode of pain.

Not on the world I love bestow,
Passing flowers that blow and die;
       Follow not you the spacious track
       That turns your back to God most high.

And love your neighbor as yourself,
(not for wealth your love should be),
       But a greater love than every love

Give God above who loves you.

He shall not see the abode of pain
Whose mercies rain on poor folk still:
      Alms, fastings, prayers, must aid the soul;
      your blood control, control your will.

Shun folly, shun greed, shun sensual fires,
(eager desires of those enslaved),
      Anger and pride and hatred shun,
      'Til heaven be won, 'til you be saved.

A Psalm, read or recited

Holy Lord,
Under my thoughts may I God-thoughts find.
Half of my sins escape my mind.
      For what I said, or did not say,
      Pardon me, O Lord, I pray.

A Scriptural Selection, read aloud or quietly

O Lord, Jesus the Christ,
If I were in Heaven my harp I would sound
With apostles and angels and saints all around,
      Praising and thanking the Son who is crowned,
      May the poor race of Eve for that heaven be bound!

Holy Lord,
Since hell each soul pursues each day,
Man and woman, 'til life does end,
      Be not deceived, as others may,
      Remember what I say, my Friend.

To him, our King, to Mary's son,
Who did not shun the evil death,
      Since he our goal is, to him alone,
      Commit your soul, your life, your breath.

O Holy Lord,

God with the Father and the Spirit,
For me is many a snare designed,
To fill my mind with doubts and fears;
    Far from the land of holy saints,
    I dwell within my vale of tears.
Let faith, let hope, let love —
Traits far above the cold world's way —
    With patience, humility, and awe,
    Become my guides from day to day.

I acknowledge, the evil I have done.
From the day of my birth till the day of my death,
    Through the sight of my eyes,
Through the hearing of my ears,
    Through the sayings of my mouth,
Through the thoughts of my heart,
    Through the touch of my hands,
Through the course of my way,
    Through all I said and did not,
Through all I promised and fulfilled not,
    Through all the laws and holy commandments I broke.
I ask even now absolution of you,
    For fear I may have never asked it as was right,
    And that I might not live to ask it again,

O Holy Lord, my King in Heaven,
May you not let my soul stray from you,
May you keep me in a good state,
    May you turn me toward what is good to do,
    May you protect me from dangers, small and great.
May you fill my eyes with tears of repentance,
    So I may avoid the sinner's awful sentence.
May the Grace of the God for ever be with me,
    And whatever my needs, may the Triune God give me.

Select one of the following options for the Lord's Prayer.

Option A

O Jesus Christ,

Lord of heaven and earth,
Help me pray as you yourself taught:
> "Our Father in heaven,
> hallowed be your name.
> Your kingdom come.
> Your will be done,
> on earth as it is in heaven.
> Give us this day our daily bread.
> And forgive us our debts,
> as we also have forgiven our debtors.
> And do not bring us to the time of trial,
> but rescue us from the evil one."
> (Matthew 6: 9-13)

From the foes of my land,
from the foes of my faith,
From the foes who would us dissever,
> O Lord, preserve me, in life and in death,
> With the Sign of the Cross for ever.
> For the kingdom, the power, and the glory
> are yours now and for ever. Amen.

Please proceed with "I beseech you, O Lord...," found after Option B.

Option B

O Jesus Christ,
Lord of heaven and earth,
Help me pray as you yourself taught:
> Our Father in heaven,
> hallowed be your name,
> your kingdom come,
> your will be done,
> on earth as in heaven.
> Give us today our daily bread.
> Forgive us our sins
> as we forgive those who sin against us.
> Lead us not into temptation
> but deliver us from evil.

From the foes of my land,

from the foes of my faith,
From the foes who would us dissever,
>O Lord, preserve me, in life and in death,
>With the Sign of the Cross for ever.
>*For the kingdom, the power, and the glory*
>*are yours now and for ever. Amen.*

I beseech you, O Lord.
God in Heaven, unsurpassed in power and might;
>Be behind me, Be on my left,
>Be before me, Be on my right!
Against each danger, you are my help;
In distress, upon you I call.
>In dark times, may you sustain me
>And lift me up again when I fall.
Lord over heaven and of earth,
You know my offenses.
>Yet, listening to my pleadings,
>You guide me away from sinful pretenses.
Lord of all creation and the many creatures,
You bestow on me many earthly treasures.
>Revealing love in each life and season,
>You share with me heavenly pleasures.
May you arouse me
In moments both of joy and of strife;
>Most holy Lord, bring me new life!

A Hymn, sung or heard (optional)

O Jesus Christ,
>Lord of heaven and earth,
>You are my riches, my store, my provision,
My star through the years
When troubles rend me,
>Through times of strife and tears,
>Sweet Jesus, defend me.

Hail, heaven's eternal glory, to you I sing
Who unto all the blessed hope did bring.
>Born of the Virgin, chaste and pure,

And of our Heavenly Father most sure.

Give us your right hand, Lord, that we may rise,
Make clean our hearts and purify our eyes,
    Like blazing torches let our song of praise
    And gratitude ascend against the skies.

***End this time of prayer by taking some time to bring to mind
the various ways God shields you from harm or guides you through
the world's tumult. Then, when you are ready, conclude by saying:***

O Holy Lord, King in Heaven,
I place myself at the edge of your grace,
    On the floor of your house myself I place,
And to banish the sin of my heart away,
    I lower my knee to you this day.
Through life's torrents of pain may you bring me whole,
    And, O Lord Jesus Christ, preserve also my soul. Amen.

2.9   To The Fount Of Life Eternal

a prayer of praise and gratitude for Christ's love

Take a moment to quiet your spirit, becoming completely present to this time and place. Allow all other thoughts and concerns to fall away as you come into the presence of God. Then, when you are ready, begin.

To the fount of life eternal
Longs my thirsting soul to rise,
Longs to break the carnal prison
      Where the darkness holds its eyes,
      Weeps and wanders like an exile,
      Yearning for its native skies.

O, when bowed beneath the burdens
And the labors of the day,
      Comes the dream of one's lost glory
      Shining sweet with heavenly ray,
Present grief but swells the longing
      For the blessings cast away.

A Hymn, sung or heard (optional)

To you, O Christ, my prayers shall rise,
With tears of sorrow blending;
      Come to my help, O you Holy One,
      On my dark night descending.

My heart shall in you find its rest,
And e'en in dreams shall praise your love;
      And with each rising of the sun,
      New songs shall raise to you above.

Impart a noble life, and may
My spirit's warmth be heightened.
      Bid night depart, and with your love,
      O, may my life be brightened.

In hymns I pay my vows to you:
At every hour to you I pray,
       Erase the many sins I have made
       And allow me with you to stay.

You are my Lord, ever most high,
You guide my path by your grace.
       May I always serve your intentions
       And your desires fully embrace.

A Psalm, read or recited

Holy Lord,
Under my thoughts may I God-thoughts find.
Half of my sins escape my mind.
       For what I said, or did not say,
       Pardon me, O Lord, I pray.

A Scriptural Selection, read aloud or quietly

O Lord, Jesus the Christ,
If I were in Heaven my harp I would sound
With apostles and angels and saints all around,
       Praising and thanking the Son who is crowned,
       May the poor race of Eve for that heaven be bound!

Holy Lord,
A reckoning-day for my actions comes,
The winnowing day of the wheat and chaff,
       I must account for each pledge and promise
       Of my living and labouring on your behalf.

Not with flattery, not with lies,
Not with pride nor haughty tone,
       Is it right for me to become Christ's friendship
       With but the love of God alone.

O Holy Lord,
       God with the Father and the Spirit,

For me is many a snare designed,
To fill my mind with doubts and fears;
      Far from the land of holy saints,
      I dwell within my vale of tears.
Let faith, let hope, let love —
Traits far above the cold world's way —
      With patience, humility, and awe,
      Become my guides from day to day.

I acknowledge, the evil I have done.
From the day of my birth till the day of my death,
      Through the sight of my eyes,
Through the hearing of my ears,
      Through the sayings of my mouth,
Through the thoughts of my heart,
      Through the touch of my hands,
Through the course of my way,
      Through all I said and did not,
Through all I promised and fulfilled not,
      Through all the laws and holy commandments I broke.
I ask even now absolution of you,
      For fear I may have never asked it as was right,
      And that I might not live to ask it again,

O Holy Lord, my King in Heaven,
May you not let my soul stray from you,
May you keep me in a good state,
      May you turn me toward what is good to do,
      May you protect me from dangers, small and great.
May you fill my eyes with tears of repentance,
      So I may avoid the sinner's awful sentence.
May the Grace of the God for ever be with me,
      And whatever my needs, may the Triune God give me.

Select one of the following options for the Lord's Prayer.

Option A

O Jesus Christ,
Lord of heaven and earth,

Help me pray as you yourself taught:

> "Our Father in heaven,
> hallowed be your name.
> Your kingdom come.
> Your will be done,
> on earth as it is in heaven.
> Give us this day our daily bread.
> And forgive us our debts,
> as we also have forgiven our debtors.
> And do not bring us to the time of trial,
> but rescue us from the evil one."
> (Matthew 6: 9-13)

From the foes of my land,
from the foes of my faith,
From the foes who would us dissever,

> O Lord, preserve me, in life and in death,
> With the Sign of the Cross for ever.
> For the kingdom, the power, and the glory
> are yours now and for ever. Amen.

Please proceed with "I beseech you, O Lord...," found after Option B.

Option B

O Jesus Christ,
Lord of heaven and earth,
Help me pray as you yourself taught:

> Our Father in heaven,
> hallowed be your name,
> your kingdom come,
> your will be done,
> on earth as in heaven.
> Give us today our daily bread.
> Forgive us our sins
> as we forgive those who sin against us.
> Lead us not into temptation
> but deliver us from evil.

From the foes of my land,
from the foes of my faith,

From the foes who would us dissever,
>O Lord, preserve me, in life and in death,
>With the Sign of the Cross for ever.
>*For the kingdom, the power, and the glory*
>*are yours now and for ever. Amen.*

I beseech you, O Lord.
God in Heaven, unsurpassed in power and might;
>Be behind me, Be on my left,
>Be before me, Be on my right!
Against each danger, you are my help;
In distress, upon you I call.
>In dark times, may you sustain me
>And lift me up again when I fall.
Lord over heaven and of earth,
You know my offenses.
>Yet, listening to my pleadings,
>You guide me away from sinful pretenses.
Lord of all creation and the many creatures,
You bestow on me many earthly treasures.
>Revealing love in each life and season,
>You share with me heavenly pleasures.
May you arouse me
In moments both of joy and of strife;
>Most holy Lord, bring me new life!

A Hymn, sung or heard (optional)

O Jesus Christ,
>Lord of heaven and earth,
>You are my riches, my store, my provision,
My star through the years
When troubles rend me,
>Through times of strife and tears,
>Sweet Jesus, defend me.

O Most Holy Lord,
Happy is that blessed spirit
Who beholds its maker nigh,
>Sees the Ruler of creation

On the throne of majesty,
Marshalling the stars and planets
In their courses through the sky.

Fill my soul with strength and vigor
In my warfare here below;
    Be your name to me a bulwark
    In my struggle with the foe;
And your sweet reward hereafter
On my soul, dear Lord, bestow.

***End this time of prayer by taking some time to bring to mind
the various ways God shields you from harm or guides you through
the world's tumult. Then, when you are ready, conclude by saying:***

O Holy Lord, King in Heaven,
I place myself at the edge of your grace,
    On the floor of your house myself I place,
And to banish the sin of my heart away,
    I lower my knee to you this day.
Through life's torrents of pain may you bring me whole,
    And, O Lord Jesus Christ, preserve also my soul. Amen.

From Passion to Resurrection

a prayer of praise, gratitude and victory

Take a moment to quiet your spirit, becoming completely present to this time and place. Allow all other thoughts and concerns to fall away as you come into the presence of God. Then, when you are ready, begin.

Dear God of mercy and of power,
Bowed at your feet in prayer and love
    I am; send down your heavenly dower,
    The Spirit's largess, from above.

As you have filled my life with light,
And oped my heart to your grace,
    So guide me ever in your might,
    And fit me for your dwelling-place.

A Hymn, sung or heard (optional)

Tell, my tongue, the glorious conflict,
Crowned with victory nobly won;
    More than all the spoils of battle,
    Praise the triumph of God's Son;
How by death the crown of conquest
    Graced Him when the strife was done.

Grieving sore o'er Eden's sorrow
When our race in Adam fell;
    And the fatal fruit he tasted,
    Welcomed sin, and death, and hell;
God ordained a tree in Zion,
    Eden's poison to dispel.

In the work of our Redemption
Wisdom met the tempter's foils;
    On the ground he claimed, the Victor
    Fought, and bore away the spoils;

And the bane became the blessing,
        Freedom sprang amid his toils.

From the bosom of the Father,
Where He shared the regal crown,
        At the time by God appointed,
        Came the world's Creator down
God incarnate, born of a Virgin,
        Shorn of glory and renown.

A Psalm, read or recited

Holy Lord,
Under my thoughts may I God-thoughts find.
Half of my sins escape my mind.
        For what I said, or did not say,
        Pardon me, O Lord, I pray.

A Scriptural Selection, read aloud or quietly

O Lord, Jesus the Christ,
If I were in Heaven my harp I would sound
With apostles and angels and saints all around,
        Praising and thanking the Son who is crowned,
        May the poor race of Eve for that heaven be bound!

All hail to you, Body of Christ,
All hail, King of Heaven's lights,
        All hail, O Holy Trinity,
        All hail to you you Right of Rights.

All hail to you, blood and flesh,
All hail to you, king of good,
        No more be angry with my soul,
        But wash it in your precious blood.

No more be angry with my soul,
But cleanse it by your gracious might,
        A hundred welcomes, God and man,
        Both now and when the Death shall smite.

O Holy Lord,
> God with the Father and the Spirit,
For me is many a snare designed,
To fill my mind with doubts and fears;
>> Far from the land of holy saints,
>> I dwell within my vale of tears.
Let faith, let hope, let love —
Traits far above the cold world's way —
>> With patience, humility, and awe,
>> Become my guides from day to day.

I acknowledge, the evil I have done.
From the day of my birth till the day of my death,
>> Through the sight of my eyes,
Through the hearing of my ears,
>> Through the sayings of my mouth,
Through the thoughts of my heart,
>> Through the touch of my hands,
Through the course of my way,
>> Through all I said and did not,
Through all I promised and fulfilled not,
>> Through all the laws and holy commandments I broke.
I ask even now absolution of you,
>> For fear I may have never asked it as was right,
>> And that I might not live to ask it again,

O Holy Lord, my King in Heaven,
May you not let my soul stray from you,
May you keep me in a good state,
>> May you turn me toward what is good to do,
>> May you protect me from dangers, small and great.
May you fill my eyes with tears of repentance,
>> So I may avoid the sinner's awful sentence.
May the Grace of the God for ever be with me,
>> And whatever my needs, may the Triune God give me.

Select one of the following options for the Lord's Prayer.

Option A

O Jesus Christ,
Lord of heaven and earth,
Help me pray as you yourself taught:
    "Our Father in heaven,
    hallowed be your name.
    Your kingdom come.
    Your will be done,
    on earth as it is in heaven.
    Give us this day our daily bread.
    And forgive us our debts,
    as we also have forgiven our debtors.
    And do not bring us to the time of trial,
    but rescue us from the evil one."
    (Matthew 6: 9-13)
From the foes of my land,
from the foes of my faith,
From the foes who would us dissever,
    O Lord, preserve me, in life and in death,
    With the Sign of the Cross for ever.
    For the kingdom, the power, and the glory
    are yours now and for ever. Amen.

Please proceed with "I beseech you, O Lord...," found after Option B.

Option B

O Jesus Christ,
Lord of heaven and earth,
Help me pray as you yourself taught:
    Our Father in heaven,
    hallowed be your name,
    your kingdom come,
    your will be done,
    on earth as in heaven.
    Give us today our daily bread.
    Forgive us our sins
    as we forgive those who sin against us.
    Lead us not into temptation

but deliver us from evil.
From the foes of my land,
from the foes of my faith,
From the foes who would us dissever,
    O Lord, preserve me, in life and in death,
    With the Sign of the Cross for ever.
    For the kingdom, the power, and the glory
    are yours now and for ever. Amen.

I beseech you, O Lord.
God in Heaven, unsurpassed in power and might;
    Be behind me, Be on my left,
    Be before me, Be on my right!
Against each danger, you are my help;
In distress, upon you I call.
    In dark times, may you sustain me
    And lift me up again when I fall.
Lord over heaven and of earth,
You know my offenses.
    Yet, listening to my pleadings,
    You guide me away from sinful pretenses.
Lord of all creation and the many creatures,
You bestow on me many earthly treasures.
    Revealing love in each life and season,
    You share with me heavenly pleasures.
May you arouse me
In moments both of joy and of strife;
    Most holy Lord, bring me new life!

A Hymn, sung or heard (optional)

O Jesus Christ,
    Lord of heaven and earth,
    You are my riches, my store, my provision,
My star through the years
When troubles rend me,
    Through times of strife and tears,
    Sweet Jesus, defend me.

"Forevermore hosanna sing,

To David's Son, our conquering King;
        To you be ever love and laud
        Who earns in the name of God."

To you shall rise the song and psalm,
O Victim meek, O spotless Lamb,
        Whose blood has washed all earthly taints
        From the white vestments of the saints.

End this time of prayer by taking some time to bring to mind the various ways God shields you from harm or guides you through the world's tumult. Then, when you are ready, conclude by saying:

O Holy Lord, King in Heaven,
I place myself at the edge of your grace,
        On the floor of your house myself I place,
And to banish the sin of my heart away,
        I lower my knee to you this day.
Through life's torrents of pain may you bring me whole,
    And, O Lord Jesus Christ, preserve also my soul. Amen.

a penitent's prayer on Jesus' Passion (Last Supper)

Take a moment to quiet your spirit, becoming completely present to this time and place. Allow all other thoughts and concerns to fall away as you come into the presence of God. Then, when you are ready, begin.

Let earth and heaven rejoice and sing
The supper of our Lord and King,
      Who cleansed our souls from sin, and gave
      The living bread to heal and save.
Let earth and heaven rejoice and sing
      That supper of our Lord and King.

The Maker of the world, that night,
With wondrous mystery and might,
      Brought to the soul her heavenly meat,
      His blood to drink, his flesh to eat;
He cleansed our souls from sin and gave
      The living bread to heal and save.

A Hymn, sung or heard (optional)

Thus the work of our salvation
Was by law divine ordained,
      Thus by good to ill opposing,
      Was the tempter's power restrained;
Whence the evil, thence the healing,
      Whence came death true life is gained.

In his holy hour the Saviour
From the halls of heaven is come.
      Takes the flesh of human nature;
      So to save the flesh from doom;
Born as man, the world's Creator
      Issues from a virgin's womb.

In a stable poor and lowly,
He, a tender child is born,
With a manger for a cradle,
Our Redeemer lies forlorn;
Swathing him in bands, the mother
Shields the Babe from shame and scorn.

Thirty years are soon completed,
And the day of woe is nigh;
Comes the hour of man's redemption,
When the Christ is doomed to die;
On the cross, a lamb, uplifted,
Lo! the Lord of earth and sky!

With a crown of thorns they crown him,
And they nail him to the wood,
With a lance they pierce his body
Whence the water and the blood
Flow, till ocean, earth and heaven
Bathe in the redeeming flood.

A Psalm, read or recited

Holy Lord,
Under my thoughts may I God-thoughts find.
Half of my sins escape my mind.
For what I said, or did not say,
Pardon me, O Lord, I pray.

A Scriptural Selection, read aloud or quietly

O Lord, Jesus the Christ,
If I were in Heaven my harp I would sound
With apostles and angels and saints all around,
Praising and thanking the Son who is crowned,
May the poor race of Eve for that heaven be bound!

O Jesus, sorely suffering
Rent by your Passion's pain,
And in un-torn offering,

Slain as among the slain,
Scoffed at, despised, neglected,
Tortured by cruel men,
    Trembling to be rejected
    I turn to you again.

O Holy Lord,
    God with the Father and the Spirit,
For me is many a snare designed,
To fill my mind with doubts and fears;
    Far from the land of holy saints,
    I dwell within my vale of tears.
Let faith, let hope, let love —
Traits far above the cold world's way —
    With patience, humility, and awe,
    Become my guides from day to day.

I acknowledge, the evil I have done.
From the day of my birth till the day of my death,
    Through the sight of my eyes,
Through the hearing of my ears,
    Through the sayings of my mouth,
Through the thoughts of my heart,
    Through the touch of my hands,
Through the course of my way,
    Through all I said and did not,
Through all I promised and fulfilled not,
    Through all the laws and holy commandments I broke.
I ask even now absolution of you,
    For fear I may have never asked it as was right,
    And that I might not live to ask it again,

O Holy Lord, my King in Heaven,
May you not let my soul stray from you,
May you keep me in a good state,
    May you turn me toward what is good to do,
    May you protect me from dangers, small and great.
May you fill my eyes with tears of repentance,
    So I may avoid the sinner's awful sentence.
May the Grace of the God for ever be with me,

And whatever my needs, may the Triune God give me.

Select one of the following options for the Lord's Prayer.

Option A

O Jesus Christ,
Lord of heaven and earth,
Help me pray as you yourself taught:
> *"Our Father in heaven,*
> *hallowed be your name.*
> *Your kingdom come.*
> *Your will be done,*
> *on earth as it is in heaven.*
> *Give us this day our daily bread.*
> *And forgive us our debts,*
> *as we also have forgiven our debtors.*
> *And do not bring us to the time of trial,*
> *but rescue us from the evil one."*
> *(Matthew 6: 9-13)*

From the foes of my land,
from the foes of my faith,
From the foes who would us dissever,
> O Lord, preserve me, in life and in death,
> With the Sign of the Cross for ever.
> *For the kingdom, the power, and the glory*
> *are yours now and for ever. Amen.*

Please proceed with "I beseech you, O Lord...," found after Option B.

Option B

O Jesus Christ,
Lord of heaven and earth,
Help me pray as you yourself taught:
> *Our Father in heaven,*
> *hallowed be your name,*
> *your kingdom come,*
> *your will be done,*

on earth as in heaven.
Give us today our daily bread.
Forgive us our sins
as we forgive those who sin against us.
Lead us not into temptation
but deliver us from evil.
From the foes of my land,
from the foes of my faith,
From the foes who would us dissever,
> O Lord, preserve me, in life and in death,
> With the Sign of the Cross for ever.
> *For the kingdom, the power, and the glory*
> *are yours now and for ever. Amen.*

I beseech you, O Lord.
God in Heaven, unsurpassed in power and might;
> Be behind me, Be on my left,
> Be before me, Be on my right!
Against each danger, you are my help;
In distress, upon you I call.
> In dark times, may you sustain me
> And lift me up again when I fall.
Lord over heaven and of earth,
You know my offenses.
> Yet, listening to my pleadings,
> You guide me away from sinful pretenses.
Lord of all creation and the many creatures,
You bestow on me many earthly treasures.
> Revealing love in each life and season,
> You share with me heavenly pleasures.
May you arouse me
In moments both of joy and of strife;
> Most holy Lord, bring me new life!

A Hymn, sung or heard (optional)

O Jesus Christ,
> Lord of heaven and earth,
> You are my riches, my store, my provision,
My star through the years

When troubles rend me,
> Through times of strife and tears,
> Sweet Jesus, defend me.

O Christ, our everlasting Light,
You the glory of the starry sky,
> Illume the darkness of our night,
> Quicken our breasts and purify.

O, save us from insidious snares,
Protect us from the dangerous foe,
> Guard, lest we stumble unawares,
> And let our sleep no evil know.

Keep you our hearts forever pure,
Increase our faith, our will with you combine.
> Be with us your protection sure,
> Save by your power and love divine.

End this time of prayer by taking some time to bring to mind the various ways God shields you from harm or guides you through the world's tumult. Then, when you are ready, conclude by saying:

O Holy Lord, King in Heaven,
I place myself at the edge of your grace,
> On the floor of your house myself I place,
And to banish the sin of my heart away,
> I lower my knee to you this day.
Through life's torrents of pain may you bring me whole,
> And, O Lord Jesus Christ, preserve also my soul. Amen.

3.3   From Out The Ancient Garden Came

a penitent's prayer on Jesus' Passion (Gethesame)

Take a moment to quiet your spirit, becoming completely present to this time and place. Allow all other thoughts and concerns to fall away as you come into the presence of God. Then, when you are ready, begin.

From out the ancient garden came,
By disobedience, death and shame;
>   But from the new come life and light
>   Where Jesus prayed in the night.

The woe of all the world he feels,
While faint upon the ground he kneels;
>   His great heart trembles with the pain,
>   Till blood-drops ooze from every vein.

A Hymn, sung or heard (optional)

Thirty years by God appointed,
And there dawns the woeful day,
>   When the great Redeemer girds Him
>   For the tumult of the fray;
And upon the cross uplifted,
>   Bears our load of guilt away.

Ah! 'tis bitter gall He drinks,
When His heart in anguish fails;
>   From the thorns His life-blood trickles,
>   From the spear wound and the nails;
But that crimson stream for cleansing,
>   O'er creation wide prevails.

Faithful Cross! in all the woodland,
Stands not a nobler tree;
>   In thy leaf, and flower, and fruitage,
>   None can e'er thy equal be;

Sweet the wood, and sweet the iron,
Sweet the load hung upon you, holy tree.

Noble tree! unbend thy branches,
Let thy stubborn fibres bend,
    Cast your native rigour from you,
    Be a gentle, loving friend;
Bear Him in your arms, and softly,
    Christ, the King eternal, tend.

Only you could bear the burden
Of the ransom of our race;
    Only you could be a refuge,
    Like the ark, a hiding-place,
By the sacred blood anointed,
    Of the Covenant of Grace.

A Psalm, read or recited

Holy Lord,
Under my thoughts may I God-thoughts find.
Half of my sins escape my mind.
    For what I said, or did not say,
    Pardon me, O Lord, I pray.

A Scriptural Selection, read aloud or quietly

O Lord, Jesus the Christ,
If I were in Heaven my harp I would sound
With apostles and angels and saints all around,
    Praising and thanking the Son who is crowned,
    May the poor race of Eve for that heaven be bound!

O Jesus sore-suffering,
Martyr of pain,
    You were offered, an offering,
    Slain with the slain,
Despised and rejected,
To be mocked among men,
    May my soul be protected

From sin and from stain.

O Holy Lord,
     God with the Father and the Spirit,
For me is many a snare designed,
To fill my mind with doubts and fears;
     Far from the land of holy saints,
     I dwell within my vale of tears.
Let faith, let hope, let love —
Traits far above the cold world's way —
     With patience, humility, and awe,
     Become my guides from day to day.

I acknowledge, the evil I have done.
From the day of my birth till the day of my death,
     Through the sight of my eyes,
Through the hearing of my ears,
     Through the sayings of my mouth,
Through the thoughts of my heart,
     Through the touch of my hands,
Through the course of my way,
     Through all I said and did not,
Through all I promised and fulfilled not,
     Through all the laws and holy commandments I broke.
I ask even now absolution of you,
     For fear I may have never asked it as was right,
     And that I might not live to ask it again,

O Holy Lord, my King in Heaven,
May you not let my soul stray from you,
May you keep me in a good state,
     May you turn me toward what is good to do,
     May you protect me from dangers, small and great.
May you fill my eyes with tears of repentance,
     So I may avoid the sinner's awful sentence.
May the Grace of the God for ever be with me,
     And whatever my needs, may the Triune God give me.

Select one of the following options for the Lord's Prayer.

Option A

O Jesus Christ,
Lord of heaven and earth,
Help me pray as you yourself taught:
> *"Our Father in heaven,*
> *hallowed be your name.*
> *Your kingdom come.*
> *Your will be done,*
> *on earth as it is in heaven.*
> *Give us this day our daily bread.*
> *And forgive us our debts,*
> *as we also have forgiven our debtors.*
> *And do not bring us to the time of trial,*
> *but rescue us from the evil one."*
> *(Matthew 6: 9-13)*

From the foes of my land,
from the foes of my faith,
From the foes who would us dissever,
> O Lord, preserve me, in life and in death,
> With the Sign of the Cross for ever.
> *For the kingdom, the power, and the glory*
> *are yours now and for ever. Amen.*

Please proceed with "I beseech you, O Lord…," found after Option B.

Option B

O Jesus Christ,
Lord of heaven and earth,
Help me pray as you yourself taught:
> *Our Father in heaven,*
> *hallowed be your name,*
> *your kingdom come,*
> *your will be done,*
> *on earth as in heaven.*
> *Give us today our daily bread.*
> *Forgive us our sins*
> *as we forgive those who sin against us.*

Lead us not into temptation
but deliver us from evil.
From the foes of my land,
from the foes of my faith,
From the foes who would us dissever,
>O Lord, preserve me, in life and in death,
>With the Sign of the Cross for ever.
>*For the kingdom, the power, and the glory*
>*are yours now and for ever. Amen.*

I beseech you, O Lord.
God in Heaven, unsurpassed in power and might;
>Be behind me, Be on my left,
>Be before me, Be on my right!
Against each danger, you are my help;
In distress, upon you I call.
>In dark times, may you sustain me
>And lift me up again when I fall.
Lord over heaven and of earth,
You know my offenses.
>Yet, listening to my pleadings,
>You guide me away from sinful pretenses.
Lord of all creation and the many creatures,
You bestow on me many earthly treasures.
>Revealing love in each life and season,
>You share with me heavenly pleasures.
May you arouse me
In moments both of joy and of strife;
>Most holy Lord, bring me new life!

A Hymn, sung or heard (optional)

O Jesus Christ,
>Lord of heaven and earth,
>You are my riches, my store, my provision,
My star through the years
When troubles rend me,
>Through times of strife and tears,
>Sweet Jesus, defend me.

O Soul of Christ bless me.
O Body of Christ save me.
    O Blood of Christ satisfy me.
    O Water of Christ's side wash me.
O Passion of Christ strengthen me.
O Jesus of the Elements, hear me O Lord.
    Make a protection for me of your wounds.
    Permit me not to be separated from you
Keep me from the attack of the Adversary.
I call me to you at the time of my death.
    In hope that I may praise you
    Along with the angels
    For ever and ever. Amen.

End this time of prayer by taking some time to bring to mind the various ways God shields you from harm or guides you through the world's tumult. Then, when you are ready, conclude by saying:

O Holy Lord, King in Heaven,
I place myself at the edge of your grace,
    On the floor of your house myself I place,
And to banish the sin of my heart away,
    I lower my knee to you this day.
Through life's torrents of pain may you bring me whole,
    And, O Lord Jesus Christ, preserve also my soul. Amen.

3.4 My Eyes Should Fall In Grief

a penitent's prayer on Jesus' Passion (Trial)

Take a moment to quiet your spirit, becoming completely present to this time and place. Allow all other thoughts and concerns to fall away as you come into the presence of God. Then, when you are ready, begin.

My eyes should fall in grief, my tears should flow,
And from my deepest heart the groan of woe
      Should rise, when I remember all the pangs
      The Saviour suffered, and the mortal blow.

The savage throng the gentle Saviour brings
Before the scornful priest's false questionings;
      Delivered to the soldiers, lo, they dare
      Raise impious hands against the King of Kings.

A Hymn, sung or heard (optional)

Consider and quake, lest devils scorn you,
Repentance make, as now I warn you,
      For Christ's words be — they are words to cherish,
      "Who turns to Me shall never perish."

Alas for him who puts off repentance,
'Til the Seeker grim comes with awful sentence,
      Those who rode to-day without grief or trouble,
      To-morrow the clay upon them others shovel.

What then of your halls where guests are laughing,
What then of your balls where wines are quaffing,
      Horses in throngs, and drink in cellars,
      Men of songs and story-tellers!

Prayer should we seek, and for prayer go hunger,
For a single week in this world is longer
      Than a thousand years where the Tree of Life is,

Where in God's garden no fear nor strife is.

No sinful mind can imagine, even,
The joys he shall find in his home in heaven,
There music, and story, and mirth surround them,
Waiting for glory with glory round them.

A Psalm, read or recited

Holy Lord,
Under my thoughts may I God-thoughts find.
Half of my sins escape my mind.
For what I said, or did not say,
Pardon me, O Lord, I pray.

A Scriptural Selection, read aloud or quietly

O Lord, Jesus the Christ,
If I were in Heaven my harp I would sound
With apostles and angels and saints all around,
Praising and thanking the Son who is crowned,
May the poor race of Eve for that heaven be bound!

Holy Lord,
Each sin I have sinned
From the day of my fall,
May the One Son of Mary
Forgive me them all!
May the child who was tortured,
God-man without stain,
Guide me safe through the torments
And shoutings of pain.

O Holy Lord,
God with the Father and the Spirit,
For me is many a snare designed,
To fill my mind with doubts and fears;
Far from the land of holy saints,
I dwell within my vale of tears.
Let faith, let hope, let love —

Traits far above the cold world's way —
　　　　With patience, humility, and awe,
　　　　Become my guides from day to day.

I acknowledge, the evil I have done.
From the day of my birth till the day of my death,
　　　　Through the sight of my eyes,
Through the hearing of my ears,
　　　　Through the sayings of my mouth,
Through the thoughts of my heart,
　　　　Through the touch of my hands,
Through the course of my way,
　　　　Through all I said and did not,
Through all I promised and fulfilled not,
　　　　Through all the laws and holy commandments I broke.
I ask even now absolution of you,
　　　　For fear I may have never asked it as was right,
　　　　And that I might not live to ask it again,

O Holy Lord, my King in Heaven,
May you not let my soul stray from you,
May you keep me in a good state,
　　　　May you turn me toward what is good to do,
　　　　May you protect me from dangers, small and great.
May you fill my eyes with tears of repentance,
　　　　So I may avoid the sinner's awful sentence.
May the Grace of the God for ever be with me,
　　　　And whatever my needs, may the Triune God give me.

Select one of the following options for the Lord's Prayer.

Option A

O Jesus Christ,
Lord of heaven and earth,
Help me pray as you yourself taught:
　　　　"Our Father in heaven,
　　　　hallowed be your name.
　　　　Your kingdom come.
　　　　Your will be done,

on earth as it is in heaven.
Give us this day our daily bread.
And forgive us our debts,
as we also have forgiven our debtors.
And do not bring us to the time of trial,
but rescue us from the evil one."
(Matthew 6: 9-13)
From the foes of my land,
from the foes of my faith,
From the foes who would us dissever,
> O Lord, preserve me, in life and in death,
> With the Sign of the Cross for ever.
> *For the kingdom, the power, and the glory*
> *are yours now and for ever. Amen.*

Please proceed with "I beseech you, O Lord...," found after Option B.

Option B

O Jesus Christ,
Lord of heaven and earth,
Help me pray as you yourself taught:
> *Our Father in heaven,*
> *hallowed be your name,*
> *your kingdom come,*
> *your will be done,*
> *on earth as in heaven.*
> *Give us today our daily bread.*
> *Forgive us our sins*
> *as we forgive those who sin against us.*
> *Lead us not into temptation*
> *but deliver us from evil.*
From the foes of my land,
from the foes of my faith,
From the foes who would us dissever,
> O Lord, preserve me, in life and in death,
> With the Sign of the Cross for ever.
> *For the kingdom, the power, and the glory*
> *are yours now and for ever. Amen.*

I beseech you, O Lord.
God in Heaven, unsurpassed in power and might;
> Be behind me, Be on my left,
> Be before me, Be on my right!
Against each danger, you are my help;
In distress, upon you I call.
> In dark times, may you sustain me
> And lift me up again when I fall.
Lord over heaven and of earth,
You know my offenses.
> Yet, listening to my pleadings,
> You guide me away from sinful pretenses.
Lord of all creation and the many creatures,
You bestow on me many earthly treasures.
> Revealing love in each life and season,
> You share with me heavenly pleasures.
May you arouse me
In moments both of joy and of strife;
> Most holy Lord, bring me new life!

A Hymn, sung or heard (optional)

O Jesus Christ,
> Lord of heaven and earth,
> You are my riches, my store, my provision,
My star through the years
When troubles rend me,
> Through times of strife and tears,
> Sweet Jesus, defend me.

Jesus mine, your glorious passion
Be my stay forevermore,
> Be my strong defense in danger,
> And of love the blessed store;
you I trust in bliss and trial,
you I cherish and adore.

> Let the splendor of your features
> Rest upon me night and day;

Fill my soul with sweet affection
Driving evil thoughts away,
Keep my body free from danger,
Let no fraud my soul waylay.

End this time of prayer by taking some time to bring to mind the various ways God shields you from harm or guides you through the world's tumult. Then, when you are ready, conclude by saying:

O Holy Lord, King in Heaven,
I place myself at the edge of your grace,
On the floor of your house myself I place,
And to banish the sin of my heart away,
I lower my knee to you this day.
Through life's torrents of pain may you bring me whole,
And, O Lord Jesus Christ, preserve also my soul. Amen.

3.5   You Gave Your Life Upon The Tree

a penitent's prayer on Jesus' death upon a cross

Take a moment to quiet your spirit, becoming completely present to this time and place. Allow all other thoughts and concerns to fall away as you come into the presence of God. Then, when you are ready, begin.

You gave your life upon the tree,
Dear Jesus, my Saviour you be;
      Who denies your true divinity
      Denies also your gift to humanity.

All godless errors, proud or vain,
The false belief and murmuring strain
      Insult your love, your law profane,
      And, my Redeemer, your hope disdain.

A Hymn, sung or heard (optional)

Think of the cross of Christ each day,
Think how he suffered for all to view,
      Think of the boon his passion gave,
      Think of the grave that gapes for you.

Think of the Son of God, how He
Died on the tree our souls to save,
      Think of the nails that pierced Him through,
      Think of Him, too, in lowly grave.

Think of the spear the soldier bore,
Think how it tore His holy side,
      Think of the bitter gall for drink,
      Think of it, think for us He died.

Think upon Christ who gave His blood
Poured in a food our souls to win,
      Think of tho mingled tide that gushed

Forth at the thrust to wash our sin.

Think of repentance timely made,
Think like a shade our time flits, too,
Think upon Death with poisoned dart
Piercing the heart and body through.

A Psalm, read or recited

Holy Lord,
Under my thoughts may I God-thoughts find.
Half of my sins escape my mind.
For what I said, or did not say,
Pardon me, O Lord, I pray.

A Scriptural Selection, read aloud or quietly

O Lord, Jesus the Christ,
If I were in Heaven my harp I would sound
With apostles and angels and saints all around,
Praising and thanking the Son who is crowned,
May the poor race of Eve for that heaven be bound!

I pray unto the Son, that He
Toward me be minded still,
His will is to redeem all,
I pray that He be of my will.

I pray unto the Father most high,
With the Holy Ghost, for safety.
They, together as three in one,
My life and salvation do guarantee.

O Holy Lord,
God with the Father and the Spirit,
For me is many a snare designed,
To fill my mind with doubts and fears;
Far from the land of holy saints,
I dwell within my vale of tears.
Let faith, let hope, let love —

Traits far above the cold world's way —
      With patience, humility, and awe,
      Become my guides from day to day.

I acknowledge, the evil I have done.
From the day of my birth till the day of my death,
      Through the sight of my eyes,
Through the hearing of my ears,
      Through the sayings of my mouth,
Through the thoughts of my heart,
      Through the touch of my hands,
Through the course of my way,
      Through all I said and did not,
Through all I promised and fulfilled not,
      Through all the laws and holy commandments I broke.
I ask even now absolution of you,
      For fear I may have never asked it as was right,
      And that I might not live to ask it again,

O Holy Lord, my King in Heaven,
May you not let my soul stray from you,
May you keep me in a good state,
      May you turn me toward what is good to do,
      May you protect me from dangers, small and great.
May you fill my eyes with tears of repentance,
      So I may avoid the sinner's awful sentence.
May the Grace of the God for ever be with me,
      And whatever my needs, may the Triune God give me.

Select one of the following options for the Lord's Prayer.

Option A

O Jesus Christ,
Lord of heaven and earth,
Help me pray as you yourself taught:
      "Our Father in heaven,
      hallowed be your name.
      Your kingdom come.
      Your will be done,

on earth as it is in heaven.
Give us this day our daily bread.
And forgive us our debts,
as we also have forgiven our debtors.
And do not bring us to the time of trial,
but rescue us from the evil one."
(Matthew 6: 9-13)
From the foes of my land,
from the foes of my faith,
From the foes who would us dissever,
　　O Lord, preserve me, in life and in death,
　　With the Sign of the Cross for ever.
　　For the kingdom, the power, and the glory
　　are yours now and for ever. Amen.

Please proceed with "I beseech you, O Lord...," found after Option B.

Option B

O Jesus Christ,
Lord of heaven and earth,
Help me pray as you yourself taught:
　　Our Father in heaven,
　　hallowed be your name,
　　your kingdom come,
　　your will be done,
　　on earth as in heaven.
　　Give us today our daily bread.
　　Forgive us our sins
　　as we forgive those who sin against us.
　　Lead us not into temptation
　　but deliver us from evil.
From the foes of my land,
from the foes of my faith,
From the foes who would us dissever,
　　O Lord, preserve me, in life and in death,
　　With the Sign of the Cross for ever.
　　For the kingdom, the power, and the glory
　　are yours now and for ever. Amen.

I beseech you, O Lord.
God in Heaven, unsurpassed in power and might;
> Be behind me, Be on my left,
> Be before me, Be on my right!
Against each danger, you are my help;
In distress, upon you I call.
> In dark times, may you sustain me
> And lift me up again when I fall.
Lord over heaven and of earth,
You know my offenses.
> Yet, listening to my pleadings,
> You guide me away from sinful pretenses.
Lord of all creation and the many creatures,
You bestow on me many earthly treasures.
> Revealing love in each life and season,
> You share with me heavenly pleasures.
May you arouse me
In moments both of joy and of strife;
> Most holy Lord, bring me new life!

A Hymn, sung or heard (optional)

O Jesus Christ,
> Lord of heaven and earth,
> You are my riches, my store, my provision,
My star through the years
When troubles rend me,
> Through times of strife and tears,
> Sweet Jesus, defend me.

And so he came unto Calvary
And died nailed upon the shameful tree,
> He died burdened by all human woe,
> And yielded his pure life, to make men free.

Yea, for my miseries the cruel pain
He bore; to bring new life his life was slain;
> So let his glory ring through earth and heaven,
> Our living God and King of endless reign.

End this time of prayer by taking some time to bring to mind the various ways God shields you from harm or guides you through the world's tumult. Then, when you are ready, conclude by saying:

O Holy Lord, King in Heaven,
I place myself at the edge of your grace,
    On the floor of your house myself I place,
And to banish the sin of my heart away,
    I lower my knee to you this day.
Through life's torrents of pain may you bring me whole,
    And, O Lord Jesus Christ, preserve also my soul. Amen.

3.6   The Sad Disciples Sat In Gloom

a prayer of joy and surprise for Jesus' Resurrection

Take a moment to quiet your spirit, becoming completely present to this time and place. Allow all other thoughts and concerns to fall away as you come into the presence of God. Then, when you are ready, begin.

The sad disciples sat in gloom,
For in the grave the Crucified
      Was laid to rest; they mourned his doom,
      And shuddered o'er the death he died.

An angel to the women gave
The truth of truths: "God is not dead;
      The Lord is risen from the grave,
      And bids his flock be comforted."

A Hymn, sung or heard (optional)

You my Redeemer are, O Christ,
My heart's desire, my fervent love;
      Creator of the world, you came
      To wear our flesh, from heaven above.

'Twas love that brought you to our aid,
To bear the burden of our woe,
      To bow the head in shameful death,
      And life, immortal life, bestow.

Asunder burst the bands of hell,
The captives hailed your glorious day;
      And by your mighty triumph crowned,
      you are at God's right hand today.

O may your mercy still abound,
That, by the goodness of your grace,
      We daily o'er our sin may rise,

And see the beauty of your face.

Spring of our joy, be you, O Christ;
Hereafter shall be our great reward;
      And while the endless ages run,
      Our praises shall we duly record.

A Psalm, read or recited

Holy Lord,
Under my thoughts may I God-thoughts find.
Half of my sins escape my mind.
      For what I said, or did not say,
      Pardon me, O Lord, I pray.

A Scriptural Selection, read aloud or quietly

O Lord, Jesus the Christ,
If I were in Heaven my harp I would sound
With apostles and angels and saints all around,
      Praising and thanking the Son who is crowned,
      May the poor race of Eve for that heaven be bound!

Holy Lord,
Born of a virgin void of stain,
your birth, your death, your broken tomb,
      Cleansing and lifting man again
      Redeemed the soul from mortal doom.

Shepherd, whose love with grief condoles,
Your baptism comes, a heavenly rain,
      Bathing with grace our waking souls,
      And washing out each deadly stain.

O Holy Lord,
      God with the Father and the Spirit,
For me is many a snare designed,
To fill my mind with doubts and fears;
      Far from the land of holy saints,
      I dwell within my vale of tears.

Let faith, let hope, let love —
Traits far above the cold world's way —
> With patience, humility, and awe,
> Become my guides from day to day.

I acknowledge, the evil I have done.
From the day of my birth till the day of my death,
> Through the sight of my eyes,
Through the hearing of my ears,
> Through the sayings of my mouth,
Through the thoughts of my heart,
> Through the touch of my hands,
Through the course of my way,
> Through all I said and did not,
Through all I promised and fulfilled not,
> Through all the laws and holy commandments I broke.
I ask even now absolution of you,
> For fear I may have never asked it as was right,
> And that I might not live to ask it again,

O Holy Lord, my King in Heaven,
May you not let my soul stray from you,
May you keep me in a good state,
> May you turn me toward what is good to do,
> May you protect me from dangers, small and great.
May you fill my eyes with tears of repentance,
> So I may avoid the sinner's awful sentence.
May the Grace of the God for ever be with me,
> And whatever my needs, may the Triune God give me.

Select one of the following options for the Lord's Prayer.

Option A

O Jesus Christ,
Lord of heaven and earth,
Help me pray as you yourself taught:
> *"Our Father in heaven,*
> *hallowed be your name.*
> *Your kingdom come.*

Your will be done,
on earth as it is in heaven.
Give us this day our daily bread.
And forgive us our debts,
as we also have forgiven our debtors.
And do not bring us to the time of trial,
but rescue us from the evil one."
(Matthew 6: 9-13)
From the foes of my land,
from the foes of my faith,
From the foes who would us dissever,
 O Lord, preserve me, in life and in death,
 With the Sign of the Cross for ever.
 For the kingdom, the power, and the glory
 are yours now and for ever. Amen.

Please proceed with "I beseech you, O Lord...," found after Option B.

Option B

O Jesus Christ,
Lord of heaven and earth,
Help me pray as you yourself taught:
 Our Father in heaven,
 hallowed be your name,
 your kingdom come,
 your will be done,
 on earth as in heaven.
 Give us today our daily bread.
 Forgive us our sins
 as we forgive those who sin against us.
 Lead us not into temptation
 but deliver us from evil.
From the foes of my land,
from the foes of my faith,
From the foes who would us dissever,
 O Lord, preserve me, in life and in death,
 With the Sign of the Cross for ever.
 For the kingdom, the power, and the glory

are yours now and for ever. Amen.

I beseech you, O Lord.
God in Heaven, unsurpassed in power and might;
  Be behind me, Be on my left,
  Be before me, Be on my right!
Against each danger, you are my help;
In distress, upon you I call.
  In dark times, may you sustain me
  And lift me up again when I fall.
Lord over heaven and of earth,
You know my offenses.
  Yet, listening to my pleadings,
  You guide me away from sinful pretenses.
Lord of all creation and the many creatures,
You bestow on me many earthly treasures.
  Revealing love in each life and season,
  You share with me heavenly pleasures.
May you arouse me
In moments both of joy and of strife;
  Most holy Lord, bring me new life!

A Hymn, sung or heard (optional)

O Jesus Christ,
  Lord of heaven and earth,
  You are my riches, my store, my provision,
My star through the years
When troubles rend me,
  Through times of strife and tears,
  Sweet Jesus, defend me.

Be with us, Jesus, evermore,
Our paschal joy forever be;
  Renew our lives, our hopes restore,
  From sin and sorrow set us free.

For Christ, the King of love and might,
Has conquered death and broke the tomb;
  He leads forth to heavenly light

The souls that long have pined in gloom.

End this time of prayer by taking some time to bring to mind the various ways God shields you from harm or guides you through the world's tumult. Then, when you are ready, conclude by saying:

O Holy Lord, King in Heaven,
I place myself at the edge of your grace,
    On the floor of your house myself I place,
And to banish the sin of my heart away,
    I lower my knee to you this day.
Through life's torrents of pain may you bring me whole,
   And, O Lord Jesus Christ, preserve also my soul. Amen.

3.7   Most Clement Jesus, Tender King

a prayer of praise for Jesus' redemption of humanity

Take a moment to quiet your spirit, becoming completely present to this time and place. Allow all other thoughts and concerns to fall away as you come into the presence of God. Then, when you are ready, begin.

Most clement Jesus, tender King,
Possess our souls that, all aglow,
　　　The tongue may fitly say and sing
　　　The love that unto you I owe.

Be with me evermore, O Lord,
And let your resurrection be
　　　My paschal joy; from crimes abhorred,
　　　In loving mercy make me free.

A Hymn, sung or heard (optional)

By death on the cross was the race restored,
For vain was our endeavour;
　　　Henceforward blessed, O blessed Lord,
　　　Be the Sign of the Cross for ever.

Rent were the rocks, tho sun did fade,
The darkening world did quiver,
　　　When on the tree our Saviour made
　　　The Sign of the Cross for ever.

Therefore I mourn for him whose heart
Shall neither shrink nor shiver,
　　　Whose tears of sorrow refuse to start
　　　At the Sign of the Cross for ever.

Swiftly we pass to the unknown land,
Down like an ebbing river,
　　　But the devils themselves cannot withstand

The Sign of the Cross for ever.

When the hour shall come that shall make us dust,
When the soul and the body sever,
　　　　Fearful the fear if we may not trust
　　　　On the Sign of the Cross for ever.

A Psalm, read or recited

Holy Lord,
Under my thoughts may I God-thoughts find.
Half of my sins escape my mind.
　　　　For what I said, or did not say,
　　　　Pardon me, O Lord, I pray.

A Scriptural Selection, read aloud or quietly

O Lord, Jesus the Christ,
If I were in Heaven my harp I would sound
With apostles and angels and saints all around,
　　　　Praising and thanking the Son who is crowned,
　　　　May the poor race of Eve for that heaven be bound!

O Christ, the King of love and might,
You have conquered death and broke the tomb;
　　　　You lead me forth to heavenly light —
　　　　My soul that long has pined in gloom.

Your holy grave, a guard defended
And at the door they placed a stone,
　　　　The guarded tomb the you rended,
　　　　And death and doom are overthrown.

O Holy Lord,
　　　　God with the Father and the Spirit,
For me is many a snare designed,
To fill my mind with doubts and fears;
　　　　Far from the land of holy saints,
　　　　I dwell within my vale of tears.
Let faith, let hope, let love —

Traits far above the cold world's way —
      With patience, humility, and awe,
      Become my guides from day to day.

I acknowledge, the evil I have done.
From the day of my birth till the day of my death,
      Through the sight of my eyes,
Through the hearing of my ears,
      Through the sayings of my mouth,
Through the thoughts of my heart,
      Through the touch of my hands,
Through the course of my way,
      Through all I said and did not,
Through all I promised and fulfilled not,
      Through all the laws and holy commandments I broke.
I ask even now absolution of you,
      For fear I may have never asked it as was right,
      And that I might not live to ask it again,

O Holy Lord, my King in Heaven,
May you not let my soul stray from you,
May you keep me in a good state,
      May you turn me toward what is good to do,
      May you protect me from dangers, small and great.
May you fill my eyes with tears of repentance,
      So I may avoid the sinner's awful sentence.
May the Grace of the God for ever be with me,
      And whatever my needs, may the Triune God give me.

Select one of the following options for the Lord's Prayer.

Option A

O Jesus Christ,
Lord of heaven and earth,
Help me pray as you yourself taught:
      "Our Father in heaven,
      hallowed be your name.
      Your kingdom come.
      Your will be done,

on earth as it is in heaven.
Give us this day our daily bread.
And forgive us our debts,
as we also have forgiven our debtors.
And do not bring us to the time of trial,
but rescue us from the evil one."
(Matthew 6: 9-13)
From the foes of my land,
from the foes of my faith,
From the foes who would us dissever,
    O Lord, preserve me, in life and in death,
    With the Sign of the Cross for ever.
    For the kingdom, the power, and the glory
    are yours now and for ever. Amen.

Please proceed with "I beseech you, O Lord...," found after Option B.

Option B

O Jesus Christ,
Lord of heaven and earth,
Help me pray as you yourself taught:
    Our Father in heaven,
    hallowed be your name,
    your kingdom come,
    your will be done,
    on earth as in heaven.
    Give us today our daily bread.
    Forgive us our sins
    as we forgive those who sin against us.
    Lead us not into temptation
    but deliver us from evil.
From the foes of my land,
from the foes of my faith,
From the foes who would us dissever,
    O Lord, preserve me, in life and in death,
    With the Sign of the Cross for ever.
    For the kingdom, the power, and the glory
    are yours now and for ever. Amen.

I beseech you, O Lord.
God in Heaven, unsurpassed in power and might;
Be behind me, Be on my left,
Be before me, Be on my right!
Against each danger, you are my help;
In distress, upon you I call.
In dark times, may you sustain me
And lift me up again when I fall.
Lord over heaven and of earth,
You know my offenses.
Yet, listening to my pleadings,
You guide me away from sinful pretenses.
Lord of all creation and the many creatures,
You bestow on me many earthly treasures.
Revealing love in each life and season,
You share with me heavenly pleasures.
May you arouse me
In moments both of joy and of strife;
Most holy Lord, bring me new life!

A Hymn, sung or heard (optional)

O Jesus Christ,
Lord of heaven and earth,
You are my riches, my store, my provision,
My star through the years
When troubles rend me,
Through times of strife and tears,
Sweet Jesus, defend me.

By the cruel mob surrounded
Scourged, and crowned with thorns and wounded,
Faint with agonizing pain;
Bowed beneath your cross, forsaken,
Jeered and scorned, I see you taken
To the mount where you are slain.

Gentle Jesus, my Salvation!
You have wrought sweet reparation

To the world for pain and loss;
>   Made yourself our bulwark, shielding
>   Man from misery by yielding
>   Thy pure life upon the cross.

End this time of prayer by taking some time to bring to mind the various ways God shields you from harm or guides you through the world's tumult. Then, when you are ready, conclude by saying:

O Holy Lord, King in Heaven,
I place myself at the edge of your grace,
>   On the floor of your house myself I place,
And to banish the sin of my heart away,
>   I lower my knee to you this day.
Through life's torrents of pain may you bring me whole,
>   And, O Lord Jesus Christ, preserve also my soul. Amen.

a petition for the Risen Jesus' continuing presence

Take a moment to quiet your spirit, becoming completely present to this time and place. Allow all other thoughts and concerns to fall away as you come into the presence of God. Then, when you are ready, begin.

Eternal builder of the skies,
Dread ruler of the night and day.
> With glories you have blessed my eyes.
> To drive the stain of pride away.

To those that seem in gloom forlorn
you are a light; your scattered fold
> Now hear the herald of the morn,
> The splendour of its rays behold.

A Hymn, sung or heard (optional)

Christ, the light that shines eternal,
Light that gilds the rolling spheres,
> Dawn upon our night, and keep us
> Pure as light when day appears.

Let no tricks of Satan snare us,
Let no enemy oppress;
> Wakeful aye with garments spotless,
> May we walk life's wilderness.

Keep our hearts in your safe-keeping,
Be your flock your special care;
> In your fold in mercy tend them,
> Guard their footsteps everywhere.

Impart a noble life, and may
Our spirit's warmth be heightened.
> Bid night depart, and with your love,

O may our lives be brightened.

And our souls shall sing triumphant
When our eyes shall see your light,
      And with you in heavenly pleasures,
      O great Triune God, we delight.

A Psalm, read or recited

Holy Lord,
Under my thoughts may I God-thoughts find.
Half of my sins escape my mind.
      For what I said, or did not say,
      Pardon me, O Lord, I pray.

A Scriptural Selection, read aloud or quietly

O Lord, Jesus the Christ,
If I were in Heaven my harp I would sound
With apostles and angels and saints all around,
      Praising and thanking the Son who is crowned,
      May the poor race of Eve for that heaven be bound!

Holy Lord,
May you restrain from words of sin;
For bitter strife give calm within;
      Veil from my eyes the garish light,
      That lures the soul to darkest night.

Pure may my inmost heart remain
From evil thoughts and fancies vain;
      And may I curb my flesh control,
      That drags to earth the aspiring soul.

O Holy Lord,
      God with the Father and the Spirit,
For me is many a snare designed,
To fill my mind with doubts and fears;
      Far from the land of holy saints,
      I dwell within my vale of tears.

Let faith, let hope, let love —
Traits far above the cold world's way —
  With patience, humility, and awe,
  Become my guides from day to day.

I acknowledge, the evil I have done.
From the day of my birth till the day of my death,
  Through the sight of my eyes,
Through the hearing of my ears,
  Through the sayings of my mouth,
Through the thoughts of my heart,
  Through the touch of my hands,
Through the course of my way,
  Through all I said and did not,
Through all I promised and fulfilled not,
  Through all the laws and holy commandments I broke.
I ask even now absolution of you,
  For fear I may have never asked it as was right,
  And that I might not live to ask it again,

O Holy Lord, my King in Heaven,
May you not let my soul stray from you,
May you keep me in a good state,
  May you turn me toward what is good to do,
  May you protect me from dangers, small and great.
May you fill my eyes with tears of repentance,
  So I may avoid the sinner's awful sentence.
May the Grace of the God for ever be with me,
  And whatever my needs, may the Triune God give me.

Select one of the following options for the Lord's Prayer.

Option A

O Jesus Christ,
Lord of heaven and earth,
Help me pray as you yourself taught:
  "Our Father in heaven,
  hallowed be your name.
  Your kingdom come.

Your will be done,
on earth as it is in heaven.
Give us this day our daily bread.
And forgive us our debts,
as we also have forgiven our debtors.
And do not bring us to the time of trial,
but rescue us from the evil one."
(Matthew 6: 9-13)

From the foes of my land,
from the foes of my faith,
From the foes who would us dissever,
     O Lord, preserve me, in life and in death,
     With the Sign of the Cross for ever.
     For the kingdom, the power, and the glory
     are yours now and for ever. Amen.

Please proceed with "I beseech you, O Lord...," found after Option B.

Option B

O Jesus Christ,
Lord of heaven and earth,
Help me pray as you yourself taught:
     Our Father in heaven,
     hallowed be your name,
     your kingdom come,
     your will be done,
     on earth as in heaven.
     Give us today our daily bread.
     Forgive us our sins
     as we forgive those who sin against us.
     Lead us not into temptation
     but deliver us from evil.

From the foes of my land,
from the foes of my faith,
From the foes who would us dissever,
     O Lord, preserve me, in life and in death,
     With the Sign of the Cross for ever.
     For the kingdom, the power, and the glory

are yours now and for ever. Amen.

I beseech you, O Lord.
God in Heaven, unsurpassed in power and might;
      Be behind me, Be on my left,
      Be before me, Be on my right!
Against each danger, you are my help;
In distress, upon you I call.
      In dark times, may you sustain me
      And lift me up again when I fall.
Lord over heaven and of earth,
You know my offenses.
      Yet, listening to my pleadings,
      You guide me away from sinful pretenses.
Lord of all creation and the many creatures,
You bestow on me many earthly treasures.
      Revealing love in each life and season,
      You share with me heavenly pleasures.
May you arouse me
In moments both of joy and of strife;
      Most holy Lord, bring me new life!

A Hymn, sung or heard (optional)

O Jesus Christ,
      Lord of heaven and earth,
      You are my riches, my store, my provision,
My star through the years
When troubles rend me,
      Through times of strife and tears,
      Sweet Jesus, defend me.

Behold the golden light appears,
The blinding shadows pass away,
      That filled our souls with shuddering fears,
      And led our feeble feet astray.

Your gaze, O Lord, is on my way,
You walk a guardian by my side,
      You see my every act each day

From earliest dawn to eventide.

End this time of prayer by taking some time to bring to mind the various ways God shields you from harm or guides you through the world's tumult. Then, when you are ready, conclude by saying:

O Holy Lord, King in Heaven,
I place myself at the edge of your grace,
    On the floor of your house myself I place,
And to banish the sin of my heart away,
    I lower my knee to you this day.
Through life's torrents of pain may you bring me whole,
    And, O Lord Jesus Christ, preserve also my soul. Amen.

3.9　O You Who Seek God To Find

a petition to live as a redeemed child of God

Take a moment to quiet your spirit, becoming completely present to this moment. Allow all other thoughts and concerns to fall away as you come into the presence of God. Then, when you are ready, begin.

O you who seek God to find,
Uplift your eyes on high;
　　　For lo!, to every humble mind
　　　His glory fills the sky.

God's mighty wonders there behold,
In boundless fields of light,
　　　Sublime, eternal, and as old
　　　As heaven and ancient night.

A Hymn, sung or heard (optional)

Be present, Holy Trinity,
One glory are you, one Deity;
　　　Where'er creation's bounds extend,
　　　You are beginning without end.

The hosts of heaven your praise proclaim,
Adoring, tell your matchless fame;
　　　Earth's threefold fabric joins the song,
　　　To bless you through the ages long.

And we, your humble servants, now
To you in courteous adoration bow;
　　　Our suppliant vows and prayers unite
　　　With hymns that fill the realms of light.

One Light, we to you our homage pay,
We worship you, O triple ray;
　　　You First and Last, we speak your fame,

And every spirit lauds your name.

To the eternal loving Father, prayers we raise;
To You, the only begotten Son, we offer praise;
      And with love of the Spirit, our hearts are ablaze,
      O great Triune God, yet also One, always!

A Psalm, read or recited

Holy Triune God,
      Father, Son and Spirit
Under my thoughts may I God-thoughts find.
Half of my sins escape my mind.
      For what I said, or did not say,
      Pardon me, O Lord, I pray.

A Scriptural Selection, read aloud or quietly

O Holy God,
      Father, Son and Spirit
If I were in Heaven my harp I would sound
With apostles and angels and saints all around,
      Praising and thanking the Son *who is* crowned,
      May the poor race of Eve for that heaven be bound!

Holy Triune God,
Pure may my inmost heart remain
From evil thoughts and fancies vain;
      And may the curb my flesh control,
      That drags to earth the aspiring soul.

So, when the last stray beams of light
Shall fade before the return of night,
      Kept in the path my feet have trod,
      I shall give glory to our God.

O Holy God,
      Father, Son and Spirit
For me is many a snare designed,
To fill my mind with doubts and fears;

Far from the land of holy saints,
I dwell within my vale of tears.
Let faith, let hope, let love —
Traits far above the cold world's way —
With patience, humility, and awe,
Become my guides from day to day.

I acknowledge, the evil I have done.
From the day of my birth till the day of my death,
Through the sight of my eyes,
Through the hearing of my ears,
Through the sayings of my mouth,
Through the thoughts of my heart,
Through the touch of my hands,
Through the course of my way,
Through all I said and did not,
Through all I promised and fulfilled not,
Through all the laws and holy commandments I broke.
I ask even now absolution of you,
In the sweet name of Jesus Christ,
For fear I may have never asked it as was right,
And that I might not live to ask it again,

O Divine Majesty,
Father, Son and Spirit
May you not let my soul stray from you,
May you keep me in a good state,
May you turn me toward what is good to do,
May you protect me from dangers, small and great.
May you fill my eyes with tears of repentance,
So I may avoid the sinner's awful sentence.
May the Grace of the God for ever be with me,
And whatever my needs, may the Triune God give me.

Select one of the following options for the Lord's Prayer.

Option A

O God,
Father, Son and Spirit,

help me pray as Jesus himself taught:
> *"Our Father in heaven,*
> *hallowed be your name.*
> *Your kingdom come.*
> *Your will be done,*
> *on earth as it is in heaven.*
> *Give us this day our daily bread.*
> *And forgive us our debts,*
> *as we also have forgiven our debtors.*
> *And do not bring us to the time of trial,*
> *but rescue us from the evil one."*
> *(Matthew 6: 9-13)*

From the foes of my land,
from the foes of my faith,
From the foes who would us dissever,
> O Trinity preserve me, in life, in death,
> With the Sign of the Cross for ever.
> *For the kingdom, the power, and the glory*
> *are yours now and for ever. Amen.*

**Please proceed with "I beseech the wonderful and blessed Trinity...,"
found after Option B.**

Option B

O God,
Father, Son and Spirit,
help me pray as Jesus himself taught:
> *Our Father in heaven,*
> *hallowed be your name,*
> *your kingdom come,*
> *your will be done,*
> *on earth as in heaven.*
> *Give us today our daily bread.*
> *Forgive us our sins*
> *as we forgive those who sin against us.*
> *Lead us not into temptation*
> *but deliver us from evil.*

From the foes of my land,
from the foes of my faith,

From the foes who would us dissever,
>O Trinity preserve me, in life, in death,
>With the Sign of the Cross for ever.
>*For the kingdom, the power, and the glory*
>*are yours now and for ever. Amen.*

I beseech the wonderful and blessed Trinity,
God in Heaven, unsurpassed in power and might;
>Be behind me, Be on my left,
>Be before me, Be on my right!
Against each danger, God is my help;
In distress, upon the Divine Majesty I call.
>In dark times, may my God sustain me —
>And lift me up again when I fall.
Lord over heaven and of earth,
The Triune God knows my offenses.
>Yet, listening to my pleadings,
>Guides me away from sinful pretenses.
Lord of all creation and the many creatures,
My God bestows on me many earthly treasures.
>Revealing love in each life and season,
>My God shares with me heavenly pleasures.
May the Holy Trinity arouse me
In moments both of joy and of strife;
>God the Father, with Mary's mighty Son,
>And the noble Spirit, bring me new life!

A Hymn, sung or heard (optional)

O Divine Majesty,
Three in one Godhead, without division.
>You are my riches, my store, my provision,
My star through the years
When troubles rend me,
>Through times of strife and tears,
>O God, you defend me.

The light is yours, O Trinity, through all my years.
Your glory shines forth in the open day;
>I come to you with songs and tears;

Lift up and guide my soul, I pray.

Cleanse me from stain of sinful pride,
And warm me in your living light;
> You are my heavenly lamp, my guide;
> Shine in your sweetness, clear and bright.

> ***End this time of prayer by taking some time to bring to mind the various ways God shields you from harm or guides you through the world's tumult. Then, when you are ready, conclude by saying:***

O Holy Triune God,
Father, Son and Spirit,
I place myself at the edge of your grace,
> On the floor of your house myself I place,
And to banish the sin of my heart away,
> I lower my knee to you this day.
Through life's torrents of pain may you bring me whole,
> And, O Blessed Trinity, preserve also my soul. Amen.

Additional Prayer Exercises

two contemplative considerations of the day

These two prayerful reflections on the day — a preview and a review, both called examens — come from the spiritual teachings of the Spanish mystic Ignatius of Loyola, who developed this prayer to heighten a person's awareness of God's presence in the commonplace experiences of daily life. However, these types of prayers would have felt familiar to the ancient Celtic saints who also saw God's presence woven into the mundane events of their lives. With this in mind, the morning examen uses the Celtic practice of encircling people and places with God's protection and love — a prayer called a *caim* — and the evening examen uses the imagination to highlight the pervasive and protective presence of God that surrounds each person in the same manner as the distinctive breastplate — or *lorica* — prayers of the ancient Celtic saints.

All of these forms of prayer, whether in these examens or in their Celtic counterparts, cultivate an awareness of God's loving activity in one's day-to-day life and foster a dynamic relationship with God based on one's trust in God's guidance and protection

Used during the morning and in the evening, each examen will require 10 or 15 minutes to complete. The morning examen focuses on the coming day, allowing the person to ask for God's guidance, protection and wisdom during future meetings and activities. The evening examen looks backward, eliciting gratitude for God's gifts during the day while also inviting repentance and a desire for personal change by heightening the individual's awareness of moments of personal sinfulness. With this in mind, these two prayers are meant to be done together so they may complement each other. By balancing a cautious anticipation of a new morning with the realistic awareness of human frailty in the evening, they teach us to reach out confidently to God for love, care and forgiveness.

These exercises are designed to become habits of prayer that remain integrated into one's daily life, rather than moments where one puts his or her daily concerns aside to pray. Because of this, individuals approaching these devotions will find it helpful to:

• Memorize the Core Prayers

It will be useful to memorize the central prayers used in each of these exercises, in much the same way that the original men and women who composed these prayers used them in their own lives. While this may seem a bit daunting, be assured that the rhythm of the prayers makes it possible to memorize them quite easily. However, individuals who are not able to memorize these prayers may write them on a small card or place them in a notepad on their mobile phone so that they may consult them when they are needed. But it is important to record only the prayers so that the surrounding exercises become natural to each individual person.

• Integrate the Examens into Daily Routines

While many people set aside 10-15 minutes in a quiet space to conduct the examen, individuals may find it better to coordinate their prayerful consideration of the day — either that which is coming or which has already passed — to a daily activity, such as dressing and undressing (i.e., putting on and taking off the concerns of the day). This will take time and effort since routine daily activities are often filled with distractions, but the effort will be rewarded since the individual will always have time devoted to the examen while also rendering that daily activity sacred.

The instructions for these exercises are not intended to be a rigid set of rules. Instead, they are designed to help individuals create a framework which will ultimately be adapted to their particular needs. Each person will need to decide how much time to devote to the exercises as well as to each particular part of them. Individuals may find that certain parts of the exercises may move slightly, depending on their own desires and needs. Trust that God is present in these decisions and will make the exercises unique gifts to each individual person.

1.   Take a moment to become still. You may want to close your eyes or you might focus your attention on a specific place or object near you. Become completely focused on this present moment and allow all other concerns or problems to dissolve and fade from your consciousness.

2.   Become aware of your desire to know the fullness of God's love for you and pray for the grace to see God's actions in your life more clearly, to understand God's desires for you more accurately and to respond to God's guidance to you more generously.

3.   Then, imagine the coming day, seeing that God's love is enfolding and encircling every situation. Imagine what you will do during the morning, during the midday hours, during the afternoon, and during the evening. Allow God's love to fill these events as you turn your attention to specific moments during the day.

    (a)   In your imagination, see the remaining morning hours. Imagine the moments when you expect to be alone and when you anticipate meeting other people. Experience your thoughts while you are alone and your words while speaking with others. Ask God to reveal the divine love shaping and sustaining these moments. Then, rest awhile in the awareness of that love and consider the people you are with before encircling them in God's love and protection, saying:
            O Father who sought me,
            Encircle and protect us!

    (b)   Imagine the events and people of the coming midday. Again, see the moments when you expect to be alone and when you anticipate meeting other people. Contemplate your thoughts while you are alone and your words while speaking with others. Once more, ask God to reveal the divine love shaping and sustaining these moments. Then, rest awhile in the awareness of that love and consider the people you are with before encircling them in God's love and protection, saying:
            O Son who bought me,
            Encircle and protect us!

(c)   See the coming afternoon, imagining the moments when you expect to be alone and when you anticipate meeting other people. Consider your thoughts while you are alone and your words while speaking with others. Again, ask God to reveal the divine love shaping and sustaining these moments. Then, rest awhile in the awareness of that love and consider the people you are with before encircling them in God's love and protection, saying:

O Holy Spirit who taught me,
Encircle and protect us!

(d)   Finally, in your imagination, see the coming evening hours. Once more, imagine the moments when you expect to be alone and when you anticipate meeting other people. Contemplate your thoughts while you are alone and your words while speaking with others. Once again, ask God to reveal the divine love shaping and sustaining these moments. Then, rest awhile in the awareness of that love and consider the people you are with before encircling them in God's love and protection, saying:

O Blessed Trinity,
Encircle and protect us!

4.   Now, as you put these images aside, express your gratitude for the ways God's love will touch you in the depths of your being as it surrounds, protects and guides you in the coming day. Then, consider how you are the instrument of God's loving presence in the world and ask how you might share that love with family, friends, neighbors, colleagues or even strangers during this day.

5.   After taking time to hear God's response, conclude by praying this ancient hymn of Saint Hilary:

From heaven has fled the starry night,
And startled sleep has taken flight;
Dear God, to you, our prayers we bring;
To you rejoicing hymns we sing.

Lord, be our hearts and hopes renewed
In light and love and gratitude;
May our deeds, illumed by you, be
Worthy of your love and glory.

We praise you, Lord, forevermore;
You, with the Son my soul does adore,
And with the Spirit, three in one,
Reigning while endless ages run.
AMEN.

1.   Take a moment to become still. You may want to close your eyes or you might focus your attention on a specific place or object near you. Become completely focused on this present moment and allow all other concerns or problems to dissolve and fade from your consciousness.

2.   Become aware of God's goodness and of the many gifts that God has given you, sustaining you and the world around you. Consider the times when you do not reflect God's goodness, the times when you squander or misuse the gifts God has given to you and the times when you feel abandoned by God.

3.   Review this day in your memory. Become aware of the gifts and of the needs you have experienced during this passing day. Allow yourself to feel God's presence in the events and emotions of this day as you consider your actions and reactions during it. Ask for the grace to gratefully acknowledge the gifts you received today and to recognize with deep remorse the gifts of God you ignored during the passing day.

    (a)   Remember the beginning of this day. Did you awaken quickly or slowly? Did the day begin easily or with difficulty? Did you feel happy or sad? Relaxed or tense? As you awoke this morning, did you feel God being present to you or distant from you? Take a moment to consider these feelings as you ponder and pray:
> *O Father who wrought me,*
> *O Son who bought me,*
> *O Spirit who sought me,*
> *Yours alone let me be!*

    (b)   Remember your preparations for the day. Did you dress quickly or slowly? What did you think about as you prepared for the day? What were your feelings? Was God involved in your preparations for this day? Take a moment to consider these events and feelings as you ponder and pray:
> *O Father who wrought me,*
> *O Son who bought me,*
> *O Spirit who sought me,*

Yours alone let me be!

(c)   Remember your morning. Did you eat breakfast or go without? Remember the other events of your morning. Were you alone or with other people? What did you do? What did you think or talk about? What emotions did you feel during the morning hours? Was God present to you or distant from you during the morning? Take a moment to consider these events and feelings as you ponder and pray:

O Father who wrought me,
O Son who bought me,
O Spirit who sought me,
Yours alone let me be!

(d)   Remember your midday. What did you do? Did you eat lunch or go without? Were you alone or with other people? What did you think or talk about? Did you feel happy or sad? Relaxed or tense? Was God present or distant? Take a moment to consider these events and feelings as you ponder and pray:

O Father who wrought me,
O Son who bought me,
O Spirit who sought me,
Yours alone let me be!

(e)   Remember your afternoon. Were you alone or with other people? What did you do? What did you think or talk about? What were you feeling? Did God feel present or distant? Take a moment to consider these events and feelings as you ponder and pray:

O Father who wrought me,
O Son who bought me,
O Spirit who sought me,
Yours alone let me be!

(f)   Remember your evening. What did you do? Were you alone or with other people? What did you think or talk about? Did you feel happy or sad? Relaxed or tense? Was God present or distant? Take a moment to consider these events and feelings as you ponder and pray:

O Father who wrought me,
O Son who bought me,
O Spirit who sought me,
Yours alone let me be!

185

4.   As you put these images aside, consider the present moment. What are you feeling toward God? Allow yourself to think or say a short one-sentence prayer in response to the memories or feelings of this day. Be completely honest in this prayer since God already knows your deepest desires, joys and pains.

5.   Then, after taking a moment to allow the thoughts and feelings of your prayer to linger on your mind and in your heart, ask God to sanctify the blessings — and heal the wounds — of this passing day using these words of Saint Ambrose:

God of creation, wondrous Might,
Eternal power that all adore,
You rule the changing day and night.
Yourself unchanging are evermore.

Pour light upon my fading day,
So in my life no dusk shall be.
So death shall bring me to the ray,
With you, Lord, of heavenly glory.

Unto you, Father of Mercy,
I lift my voice in prayer and praise,
And to the Son and Spirit be
Like glory to the end of days.
AMEN.

Resources

Recommendations for Scriptural Readings

Each of these prayer sequences include a psalm and a reading from either the Old or New Testament, but the selection of these biblical passages differs according to how the prayer sequences are approached. The use of scriptural materials may be adapted or changed according to the desires of the individual or group when using the sequences as discrete moments of prayer. However, the choice to engage the sequences in a thematic cluster greatly diminishes this flexibility. So, with this in mind, it is important to consider the different roles of the scriptural readings in different uses of the prayer sequences.

Using Each Sequence Discreetly

As a collection of discrete prayers, this book provides individuals and groups with a wide range of choices in sharing their deepest desires with God. As such, individuals or groups decide upon the specific prayer sequence that is most expressive of their needs and include scriptural readings that mirror or amplify their sense of neediness before God. Yet, this process may begin either with the selection of the sequence followed by a search for the appropriate scriptural readings or with the selection of the scriptural readings followed by the selection of an appropriate prayer sequence.

In the first approach, individuals and groups begin by selecting the sequence most relevant to their perceived needs and then search for scriptural readings relevant to the chosen prayer sequence. This process may take different forms, to include:
•   Using biblical passages that are especially meaningful to the individuals or groups using the prayer sequences. This might also include collecting favorite scriptural passages from among the members of the prayer group or asking trusted soul friends and spiritual guides for their suggestions.
•   Consulting resources prepared by other people, such as online collections of biblical readings or concordances. A general search of a specific topic will create a list of readings related to the subject of your prayer, but a concordance should offer a broader context for understanding a specific biblical theme.

Both of these approaches require their own prayerfulness since it will be important to compare various biblical verses to make sure they properly address the desires presented when praying with the sequences.

Note: It is important to remember that prayer does not begin or end during formal prayer. A person's openness to God's guidance before formal periods of prayer will foster an awareness of the readings best suited to the individual's needs when using a specific sequence. Likewise, an individual's disposition during prayer will contribute to the person's ability integrate the readings into their daily life.

The second approach to finding biblical readings for these sequences involves connecting the prayer of individuals and groups to a larger church community by using the cycles of scriptural readings developed by various denominations. These cycles may be found in the lectionaries used by the different denominations. The Roman Catholic lectionary provides readings for Sunday using a three-year cycle and readings for weekdays following a two-year cycle. Many Protestant denominations use the Revised Common Lectionary, which employs a three-year cycle for both Sunday and weekday readings. Both of these lectionaries offer options coordinating the psalms to the Gospel (or a secondary reading) for each day. While this approach may seem to randomly place readings and prayer sequences together, the individuals and groups using this method should trust that quite often "God writes straight with curving lines".

However individuals or groups choose to find the scriptural materials they use with the prayer sequences, it remains very important that they take time to review the quality of their prayer. It is in this way that they will know they have found the best source of scriptural readings to sustain their use of the sequences as discrete prayers.

Using the Sequences in Thematic Clusters

While the prayer sequences in this book may be approached discretely, they also are organized in three thematic clusters intended to be approached individually or together as a part of a progression through all twenty-seven prayer sequences. These clusters invite a prayerful consideration of specific spiritual desires. This means that the choice of specific scriptural readings needed to be carefully coordinated to each prayer sequence, so individuals and groups should use the biblical selections chosen within each cluster.

Note: Since these readings are provided, it is important to read them through before approaching the sequence in which they are used. Becoming familiar with these readings beforehand will help them become organic expressions of individual or communal needs.

The first cluster— From Loss to Love — addresses the issue of sin and redemption as it leads an individual to live in God's continuing love even as we remain aware of being sinners. The readings for this cluster include:

	Psalm	Reading
1.1	Ps 20	Rom 8:28-39
1.2	Ps 103	Jn 14:15-28
1.3	Ps 8	Lk 15:11-32
1.4	Ps 36	Mt 13:24-30
1.5	Ps 139	Jer 18:1-11
1.6	Ps 32	Mt 25:31-46
1.7	Ps 138	Jn 10:1-18
1.8	Ps 145	Jn 8:2-11

| 1.9 | Ps 84 | Eph 6:10-18 |

The second cluster — From Disciple to Friend — invites an individual to become Jesus' companion and to serve in his redemptive mission. The readings for this cluster include:

	Psalm	Reading
2.1	Ps 40	Is 43:1-7
2.2	Ps 72	Heb 1:1-14
2.3	Ps 127	Rom 12:1-8
2.4	Ps 42	Lk 4:14-22
2.5	Ps 63	Jn 1:35-51
2.6	Ps 23	Gal 5:16-25
2.7	Ps 91	Mt 14:22-33
2.8	Ps 107	Lk 10:25-37
2.9	Ps 15	Jn 2:1-11

The third and final cluster — From Passion to Resurrection — invites an individual to share in the sorrow of Jesus' passion and the joy of his resurrection as well as to respond to the Risen Christ's call to build the Kingdom of God. The readings for this cluster include:

	Psalm	Reading
3.1	Ps 21	Mt 21:1-11
3.2	Ps 113	Jn 13:1-30
3.3	Ps 118	Mt 26:36-45
3.4	Ps 31	Mt 27:11-23
3.5	Ps 22	Jn 19:16-37
3.6	Ps 2	Jn 20:11-18
3.7	Ps 62	Lk 24:13-35
3.8	Ps 30	Jn 21:1-19
3.9	Ps 16	Eph 4:1-16

After making an initial journey through these three clusters, individuals and groups may decide to repeat their journey by selecting readings that are related to those which were initially proposed. This process will require a careful consideration of alternative readings related to the initial themes or topics of each prayer sequence within a specific cluster. However, in this way, individuals and groups also will be able to make these prayer clusters uniquely expressive of their specific needs and desires.

�֍

Through the careful consideration and selection of biblical readings to accompany these sequences, individuals and groups will be able to make this collection of prayers a source of solace and an expression before God of their specific holy desires. Still, it is important to remember that the many centuries of prayer woven into the fabric of this book will unite with these modern choices to create a chorus spanning all these generations of holy pilgrims. In selecting the biblical readings to be used with these prayer sequences, individuals and groups choose to participate in this communion of saints and the spiritual companionship it provides.

Some Suggestions Concerning Music

The use of music is not essential to these sequences but its inclusion — whether with or without words — may enhance the contemplative environment fostered by these prayers. However, it is important for individuals or groups approaching the sequences to find musical expressions properly suited to the prayerful atmosphere they want to create and the musical resources available to them. This requires a careful consideration of who is praying, how the prayers are conducted, the types of music that might be used during the sequences, who will sing or present the various pieces of music, and how these different elements will be coordinated without disrupting the prayers.

Individuals and small groups may find it easiest to use recorded instrumental music or songs near the beginning and end of the prayer sequences. This preserves the contemplative atmosphere of the sequences, avoiding disruptive activities during prayers while also providing opportunities for silent reflection during the musical interludes.
•   If instrumental music is used, then the individual or group should focus on deepening into a contemplative environment of the prayers at the beginning and reflectively engage the effects of prayer near the end.
•   If songs or hymns are used, then the selection used at the beginning of the sequence should deepen the participant's appreciation of the themes of the sequence and the selection at the end should heighten awareness of the participant's response to the prayer time.
While this approach allows for a wide range of music to be used, the rhythms and language of these prayer sequences invite the use of Celtic hymns and songs. Fortunately, a wide number of musicians have recorded variations of Celtic music that would be very appropriate to the sequences.

Note: Of course, if a small group is made up of musicians, they might decide to perform together during the musical interludes as an expression of their communal worship.

The use of music in larger groups should foster a prayerful environment and be presented in a manner that does not distract from the contemplative atmosphere cultivated through the prayer sequences. This involves selecting music that enhances the prayer of the participants as well as performing the musical interludes in a manner that preserves the intrinsic rhythms of the sequences.

• The songs or hymns performed near the beginning of the sequence should be thematic, echoing the theme or readings used during the prayers and helping the participants enter more deeply into their communal worship.

• On the other hand, music presented at the end of the sequence should reflect the hopes and desires expressed during the previous prayers in order to offer a sense of individual closure as the community disperses.

As with the suggestions for individuals and small groups, it is highly recommended that Celtic music be used during these moments of communal worship. With this in mind, larger groups approaching the prayer sequences might find it useful to explore Ray Simpson's *Celtic Hymn Book* and the hymns and songs available through the Iona Community's Wild Goose Resource Group.

Ultimately, however, each person or group approaching the sequences will need to find their own way of maintaining a balance between the singing, speaking and listening that they wish to include in their prayers. While these efforts may be challenging, they will be rewarding and create unique environments of prayer suited to the needs of the individuals and groups using these prayer sequences.

About the Author

A former Jesuit, **Timothy J. Ray** brings a diverse background in creative writing, cultural studies, theology and the history of ideas to his work in spiritual direction and formation. He received his Bachelor of Arts, *magna cum laude*, in a multi-disciplinary program focused on the cultural history of law and politics from Niagara University before earning, with distinction, both his Master of Fine Arts in Dramaturgy and Dramatic Criticism from Yale University and his Master of Letters in Theology from the University of Saint Andrews. In addition to preparing *Seeking our Place of Resurrection*, he has published *The Carmichael Prayerbook*, *A Journey to the Land of the Saints*, *A Pilgrimage to the Land of the Saints* and *Nurturing the Courage of Pilgrims*.

For more information about Timothy and his activities, please visit http://www.silentheron.net.

Printed in Great Britain
by Amazon

21561573R00119